Spirit Horse
of the
Rockies

Susan R. Nardinger

Copyright © 1988 by Susan R. Nardinger

All rights reserved, including the right to reproduce this book or parts thereof, in any form, except for the inclusion of brief quotations in a review.

Library of Congress Number 88-90925
ISBN 0-937959-48-0

Published by:
Spirit Horse Enterprises
415 40th St. N.
Great Falls, MT 59401

Marketing and Distribution:
Falcon Press Publishing Co., Inc.
P.O. Box 1718
Helena, Montana 59624

DEDICATION

To my family: my husband, Dan, whose fine photographs enhance this text; my boys, Phillip, Joey, and Greg, who willingly took on the household chores while I typed; my brother, Pete Schumacher, who loaned me the use of his computer; and my mother, Alice Schumacher, whose endless confidence kept my spirits high; and finally, my grandfather, A. D. Clink, who inspired me with my love of horses.

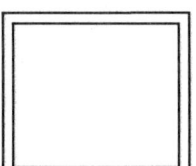

Contents

Introduction	vii
Spokane's Pedigree	ix
Preface	xi
Acknowledgments	xix
The Legend of the Spirit Horse	1
The Wrongs of Colonel Wright	5
The Armstrong Connection	13
The Round Barn	21
Bunch Grass to Blue Grass	31
Two for Five	39
Derby Dreams	45
A Classic Begins	49
Royal Derby	57
Making the News	61
Not a Fluke	69
A King's Blanket	73
Kangaroos, Derbies and Coonskins	79
Pre-Race Trials and Predictions	89
Crowds, Wagers and Tension	95
Third Time Charm	101
Horse for All Regions	109
Fire to Flickering Flame	119
Glory Enough	127
Spirituelle	137
Bibliography	145
Glossary	153
About the Author	155

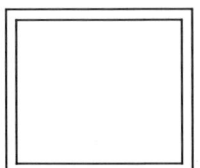 # Introduction

One of the most unique stories ever to unfold from the pages of horseracing history is the saga of Spokane. Surely each Kentucky Derby has produced a miracle tale of implausibility leading to victory, but seldom has any Thoroughbred traced a more oblique path to racing stardom than did the winner of the 1889 Kentucky Derby. This book should satisfy any student of the turf as a factual and entertaining account of the fifteenth renewal of this American classic race.

This story might have been told by a legion of other writers who would have presented the details in a more acceptable fashion. Fortunately, the Spokane story was crafted by Susan Nardinger as a real labor of love and is far more than the story of a horse. By combining all the best elements of folklore, legend, fact and her own engaging style, Susan places the reader in America at the time when it was changing from a frontier nation into a country poised to enter the twentieth century. Montana's emergence as a state, the final confinement of the American Indian, the coming of age of the great Midwestern cities; all of these events paralleled Spokane's path to greatness. This book is an adventure back to a time a century ago when an entire nation stopped to marvel at an unlikely champion from the bunchgrass region of Montana: Spokane. Susan Nardinger has done the Kentucky Derby Museum a grand favor by writing this book. I only wish each Kentucky Derby winner could be recognized in such a memorable fashion.

Randy W. Ray
Executive Director
Kentucky Derby Museum

May 10, 1988

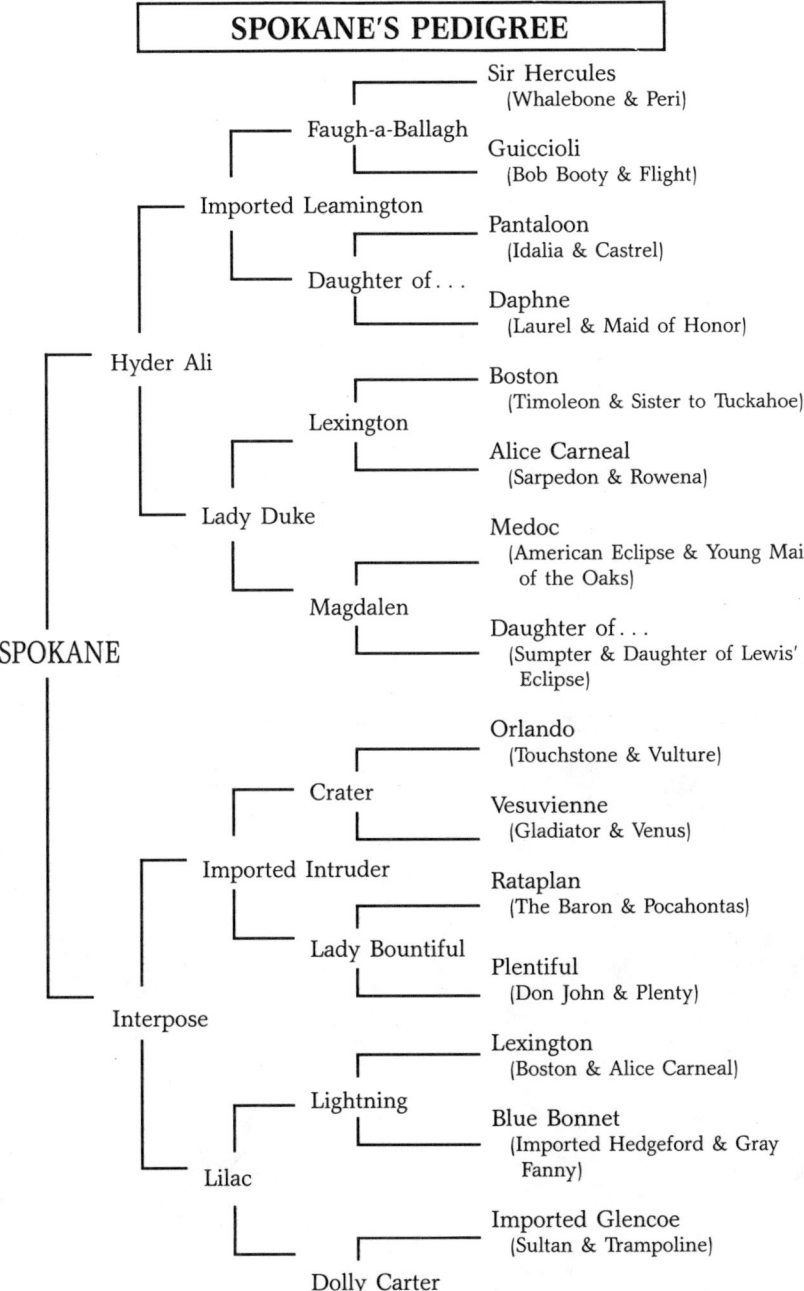

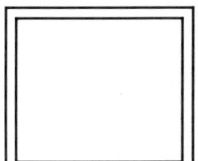 # Preface

In Montana one hundred years ago, two spectacular events occurred that inspired national recognition. In 1964, writer George McVey identified them as "Statehood and Spokane".

Today, I understand this statement. Prior to the summer of 1986, it was incomprehensible. In July of that year, I took visiting relatives to Helena, Montana, to tour the Old Governor's Mansion and Carriage House. Beautifully restored and maintained by the Montana Historical Society, the home was a "must see" for my guests.

As our young guide told of the history of the mansion, we marveled at the antique glory of our surroundings. Behind the main building, the Carriage House revealed new scenes to draw our attention. There were rich buggies, a wonderful cutter, and a magnificent carriage horse bedecked in silver-studded harness. Having been on the tour before, I always looked forward to seeing the grand horse. Even so, I was unprepared for the next words spoken by our guide. Pointing to the horse, he proclaimed, "This is Spokane, the only Montana horse to ever win the Kentucky Derby."

I have been a "horse nut" since my first encounter with a white, Hi-Ho-Silver rocking horse received on the occasion of my third birthday. As a youngster, I avidly read all the available books about horses, and I owned the largest horse collection on my block. Over a hundred proud steeds graced my bedroom shelves. My love of horses was shared by my grandfather. Together we watched these beautiful creatures at every opportunity. Kentucky Derby Day was a ritual, cherished and anticipated. We dreamed aloud of going to the Derby and of seeing a Montana horse win this, the most prestigious event in all of racing. A teenager when my grandfather passed away and left me $1,000, I hurried to purchase what I knew he wished me to own, a car and a horse.

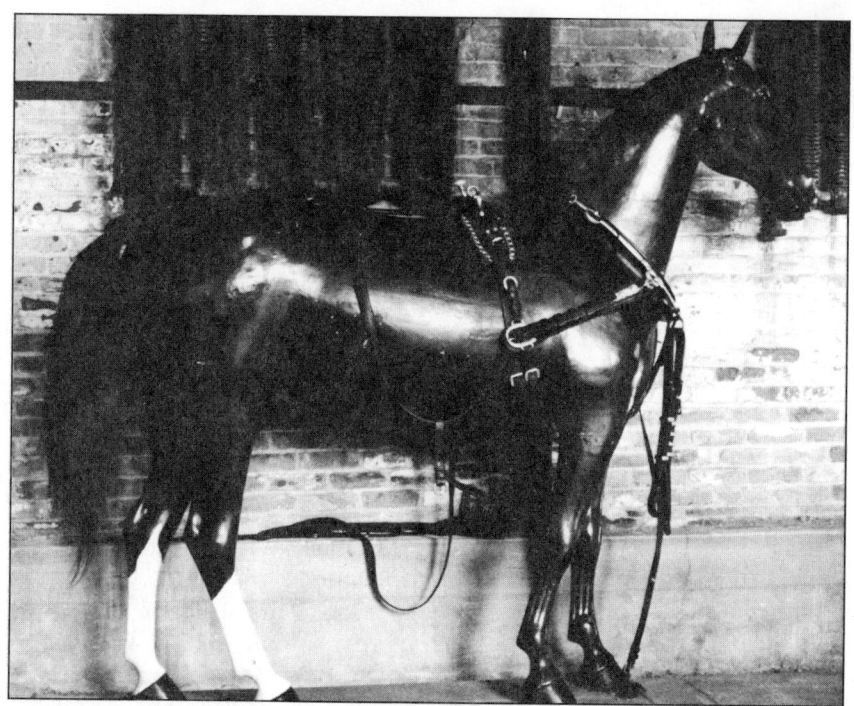

Spokane in harness at the Old Governor's Mansion, Helena, Montana. Statue owned by the Montana Historical Society, the gift of John Wall. Dan Nardinger photo.

Long ago, my blue Rambler passed into an auto graveyard, but my beautiful, black, three-quarter Arabian mare, Queen, still roams my pasture. Twenty-six years young, she demands the respect of all who board her proud back.

I stared at the Carriage House statue in disbelief. How, with all this horse savvy, had Montana's most famous steed escaped my knowledge? I taught Montana history, yet this animal hero was unknown to me! Why was this noble racer wearing a harness? Where was the plaque that told his name and described his great feat? These questions flooded my brain.

When my astonishment passed, I bombarded the poor guide with my inquiries. He told me to take the matter up with Senator Power, one of Montana's first senators, and well beyond the reaches of my curious mind. Light-heartedly, we dismissed the matter and completed our tour, but the questions, once raised, would not leave me.

It seemed as though an equine crime had been committed. I felt called to bring forth justice. Spokane deserved to take his rightful place in history. My search began.

Who was this race horse? Who owned him? Where was he foaled?

Author and son, Greg, in front of the Round Barn in August of 1986. Dan Nardinger photo.

When did he win the Kentucky Derby? Why was the Montana horse named Spokane? What happened to the great racer?

The well-kept files of the Montana Historical Society provided a beginning. The papier maché model of Spokane was ordered by Senator T.C. Power. It remained in the possession of the Power-Townsend Company of Helena until John Wall presented it to the Society in January of 1966. The statue graced a float in the Vigilante Parade of May 9, 1938. One of the local high school boys dressed as a jockey.

The round barn of Spokane's birth still stood. It was under the care of Byron Bayers of Twin Bridges. I traveled to Twin Bridges to view firsthand this unique structure. Mr. Bayers kindly opened his files to me, a stranger, and Spokane came alive.

My original plan, to write an article that would call attention to Spokane's greatness and create a demand that he be rightfully attired as a racehorse, his harness but an unpleasant memory, evaporated. For before my eyes, a story unfolded that was so significant, so haunting, and yet so contradictory that my heart cried to unlock its mysteries and tell the whole story, separating fact from fiction.

Following my trip to Twin Bridges, I journeyed to Spokane, Washington. There I discovered the reason for Spokane's name, the facts behind his legend, and the location of owner Noah Armstrong's descendants. I feasted my eyes on one of the most expensive blankets in racing history.

For many years, all trace of the blanket was lost despite every effort to find it. Finally, according to an old, torn newspaper clipping, it was discovered and placed on display in the window of Rhodes Brothers Department Store, loaned to them by Carl Armstrong, grandson of Noah. Included in this display was an oil painting of the horse. In 1941, the King's Blanket found its present home with the Eastern Washington Historical Society. Joseph Gottstein, owner of the Seattle Longacres Track, received the blanket as legatee of an estate. Knowing that the money of Spokane citizens purchased the rich robe, Mr. Gottstein made a gift of it to the Spokane Chamber of Commerce in April of 1941. On May 13 of that year, Mr. O. M. Waddell, then the curator of the Historical Society Museum, accepted the gift. The Spokane Athletic Round Table, a local civic organization, built a showcase. So housed were five items: the horse blanket, surcingle, hood, a framed and decorated horseshoe, and a picture.

The horseshoe originally sported orange and blue ribbons reflecting the colors of the Montana Stable, carefully woven through its nail holes. A handsomely printed card bearing the following inscription filled the center of the shoe: "Spokane: Winner of the Kentucky Derby, May 9, 1889. 1 1/2 mile. 118 pounds. Mile, 1:41 1/2. 1 1/4 mile, 2:09 1/2. 1 1/2 mile, 2:34 1/2. Winner of the Clark Stakes, May 14, 1889. Property of Montana Stables. Compliments of Armstrong and Hundley."

This plate, or shoe, was only one of four. Another, as evidenced by a June 8, 1889, *Great Falls Tribune* article was sent to Secretary Pope of the Helena Fair Association. Its location is unknown.

The picture mentioned is possibly a photo of a pencil sketch, or even an actual likeness of the horse taken after 1889, but so dated in honor of his accomplishments of that year.

Spokane's conquests were welcomed throughout the West, but nowhere more so than in the city of Spokane Falls, Washington Territory. This was not only his namesake, but the birthplace of his Indian legend. As one of the city's founding fathers declared, "People who never heard of Spokane Falls before now know of its existence. The victory of Spokane in the Kentucky Derby has given us our first national publicity."

Bob Johnson, Spokane sports columnist wrote in 1964, "A One-Horse Town? Maybe, But What a Horse!"

It is the natural tendency of Montanans to assume that every great racer attributed to the state's past belonged to the copper king of Anaconda, Marcus Daly. In most cases, they are right, but Spokane is an exception. Spokane belonged to pharmacist, chemist, engineer, and mining entrepreneur, Noah Armstrong. I next journeyed to Seattle, Washington, to visit with his descendants.

Hand-written documents disclosed the secrets of the " modern" barn, as well as Noah's personal feelings about the Derby victory. There were yellowed newspaper clippings, a brass nameplate, a tattered ribbon, and the family Bible. Privileged to sit in Noah's chair, I dreamed of times long ago.

In February, my family and I went camping. Luckily, the Montana winter was mild. We journeyed to Melrose, Montana, and met Ben Goody, the local historian. He took us on a tour of Glendale, present-day ghost town and former site of Noah Armstrong's silver mining operations. Here, at the Glendale cemetery, we discovered the reason for Noah's immersion into his hobby, horse racing.

Writing about a Kentucky Derby, whetted my desire to experience one. Hesitantly, aware that tickets were both rare and expensive, I made inquiries. By some miracle, on May 2, 1987, my childhood dream became reality.

The moment I beheld the twin spires of Churchill Downs, I knew that this was hallowed ground to horsemen everywhere. I was at once struck by the beauty of the area, the brightness of the tulips, the height of the fountains, the smell of the mint juleps, and the glory of the winner's circle. My breath caught as all my favorite Kentucky Derby steeds paraded through my mind: Assault, Dark Star, Swaps, Iron Liege, Northern Dancer, Lucky Debonair, Majestic Prince, Secretariat, Seattle Slew, Genuine Risk, Gato Del Sol, Swale, Ferdinand, and of course, Spokane.

Just as in 1889 when vendors hawked their wares, and crowds poured through the gates, I became a part of a living history. News of the horses flew from every quarter. Everyone was an expert on Derby Day. Some based their wagers on trivial concerns such as beauty, name, or number. Others took a more educated stance looking at post position, jockey, trainer, owner, and past performances. Everywhere came the question, "Who do you like for the Derby?"

I watched the mighty hopes of thousands thread their way onto the track. I saw sleek coats betraying stout muscles, and I knew the antonyms that are Derby: work, pleasure; tears, joy; anticipation, finality; risk, security; failure, success; obscurity, and fame. Unrelenting hope piloted dreams of boundless glory. The fireworks of fortune exploded, and a timeless Thoroughbred heritage claimed its next king.

That day, two great horses fought their way to the finish line, Alysheba and Bet Twice. Alysheba won the battle, but a rivalry began that again brought to my mind the 1889 season. With a little imagination, I pictured the Spokane and Proctor Knott duels almost one hundred years earlier, six confrontations in all. Ironically, Alysheba, I later learned, was owned in part by a Montana business woman.

Now, I understood for the first time the oft-quoted words of Irvin S. Cobb, as he struggled to describe the Kentucky Derby: "If I could do

May, 1938. Spokane's statue in the Helena, Montana, Vigilante Day Parade. Float was Sweepstakes Winner.

that I'd have a larynx of spun silver and the tongue of an angel...Until you go to Kentucky and with your own eyes behold the Derby, you ain't never been nowheres, and you ain't never seen nothin.'"

On my return home, I had to admit that even these Montana eyes watered as the strains of "My Old Kentucky Home" rolled across the grandstand. It was as though the sand driven by Spokane's hooves etched his story in my brain. Across the barrier of time, Spokane's legend called me forward.

Some Montanans do remember Spokane's triumphs. Annually in Twin Bridges at the mid-August Madison County Fair and Horse Show, they host the Spokane Memorial Handicap, a 6 1/2 furlong open race. No fancy pedigree is necessary. All are welcome.

The amazing round barn still stands. The bunch grass yet grows. The Montana air is pure and clean. Mountain streams flow free, fresh, and clear. Determined, strong-willed people populate the area. Montana has lost nothing over the past one hundred years of her existence. On the contrary, she is a young plant with deep roots growing in vision toward a future that is founded on hope and evidenced through time.

Spokane holds a record for the 1 1/2 mile Kentucky Derby that has never been broken, he was the first horse in history to win two Derbies, and his three successive wins give him the "triple crown" of his era.

I hope that Spokane's story will be a sign of promise, a beacon that lights the way for others, proof that the Spirit Horse of the Rockies lives.

Susan Nardinger
August 13, 1987

ACKNOWLEDGMENTS

Most material for this book was supplied by early day newspaper reporters. I salute their descriptive and detailed texts without which Spokane's story would not have been possible. These early day artisans plied their trade without benefit of modern photography, radio, or television.

Also, I send a special thanks to:
> Byron and Pauline Bayers;
> Herb and Elda Armstrong;
> Harriet Turner;
> Lucille Matthews;
> Ben Goody;
> Nancy Campau, Spokane Public Library;
> Larry Schoonover, Eastern Washington Historical Society;
> Randy Ray, Kentucky Derby Museum;
> Churchill Downs;
> John and Wyline Sage;
> Marianne Miller;
> Barbara Davis;
> Philip E. Von Borries;
> Theresa C. Fitzgerald, The Blood Horse;
> The Thoroughbred Record;
> The New York Jockey Club;
> Doris Waren, Keeneland Library;
> Montana Historical Society;
> Clearwater Photo of Great Falls;
> Quickest Printer, Great Falls;
> Norma Ashby;
> Connie Nicholas;
> John Wall;
> Ed Jasmin;
> Virginia City Museum;
> Great Falls Public Library;
> Madison County Courthouse;
> Skip Sherman, State Fair of Great Falls;
> Pat Greenleaf;
> Helen Fenton;
> Dan Grantier;
> Jerry Smith;
> and Bob Doerk.

To all those who responded willingly to my countless inquiries.

Thank you!!

1 The Legend Of The Spirit Horse

High in the Ruby Mountains of Montana sounds the neighing of a spirit horse. His mane blown by the breeze, his head held high, and nostrils flared, he stands ready to race and win. I see him in my mind's eye, and I feel his proud presence as I stand in the shadow of his home, an imposing round barn just north of Twin Bridges. Spokane, Child of the Sun, Spirit Horse of the Rockies, born to redeem the losses of a noble race.

The Indians of the Spokane region were men of culture and vision. They believed in the forces of good and evil. Man, they believed, possessed an eternal soul that escaped the body at death. Communication with the spirit world was considered not only possible, but probable.

Chief Tilcoax of the Palouse tribe was a brave warrior in 1858 and one not prone to seek the path of peace. Known to the white man as Wolf Necklace, he preferred the rifle to the pipe. When the "Boston men," as he called the white invaders, began to intrude on Indian lands, he urged the varied tribes to unite. Drawing together the hostile factions of Spokanes, Coeur d'Alenes, Yakimas, Palouses, and others, he ridiculed those who refused to join him, making fun of their cowardly ways.

Tilcoax promised, "I will lead my people to a glorious victory. Follow me, and your lands will belong to you forever. No white man will dare to destroy those I lead."

"White men," declared Chief Tilcoax, "break their promises. They want only gold from the breast of Amotkan, the creator, whose lands they raid without regard for forests, meadows, or wildlife."

By offering horses to entice allegiance to his cause, Tilcoax succeeded in amassing an army of fellow resistors. Together, they plotted to save a way of life and gain honor for their people. Wearing a painted face and dressed in his chiefly garb, Tilcoax led the war dance. He was not afraid of war; he welcomed it.

A wealthy man, one who owned many horses, Chief Tilcoax gave no thought to losing. That's why he was not concerned when a company of white soldiers trailed his band into the hills, causing them to abandon their valuable charges, 850 of his most prized horses. Stealing horses was sport for Tilcoax. In only a matter of days, his riches would be restored to him.

As Tilcoax watched from the high cliffs, he laughed with his fellow tribesmen. It was an amusing sight, these white soldiers wrangling his wild and proud animals. Many ropes they threw, but few caught anything but dust. Those that did succeed in trapping their prey, provided the best entertainment. The Indian horses, like their owners, put up a fierce resistance. They unseated many and outran the soldiers' mounts with ease. It was clear to the braves who looked on that these white soldiers could never continue their march while maintaining control of the stolen horses. The Indians eagerly anticipated stampeding the herd and getting not only their ponies, but those of the army's as well.

Colonel Wright viewed the return of his soldiers and their unruly booty with different eyes. This was trouble, and he knew it. Colonel Wright was not unlike Tilcoax. Wright, too, was proud and stubborn. His steel blue eyes, chiseled features, gun-metal gray hair, and stiff military posture displayed no hint of compassion. These horses could not be held in camp, and they could not be released. The only practical solution to the problems their presence created was to kill the animals. On Wright's order, the bloody slaughter began.

Soldiers, trained to love and value horses, became the instruments of their destruction. Colts were separated from their mothers and clubbed to death. Battle-hardened men wept. In obedience to command, but through tear-swollen eyes, rifles were aimed. The Indian ponies were shot. For two days, the nightmare continued. The cries of more than a hundred brood mares echoed through the stagnant air. Finally, all that remained was the stench of rotting flesh amid pools of blood, standing to dry in the warm September sun. Once a pleasant, peaceful site on the lush banks of the Spokane River where soldiers took refuge in a hostile land, Wright's camp became a place of death.

Once again, hidden by the lofty heights of their homeland, Chief Tilcoax and his followers watched, but this time they did not laugh. The wealth of Tilcoax was destroyed. His beautiful, sleek horses of the bunch grass were dead. Tilcoax never had suspected that anything so terrible might happen. This was not the way the Indian waged war. The grief-stricken chief fell to his knees, closed his eyes, and prayed to Amotkan. "Creator," he begged, "Forgive my foolish ways. To fight these white men was a mistake. Look upon my pride with pity and heal my broken heart." With these words, Chief Tilcoax collapsed and fell into a deep, trance-like sleep.

In his dream, Tilcoax saw the slaughter again. There was his favorite spotted war pony; his fleet, gray buffalo horse; his daughter's coppery colt that used to playfully beg treats at the teepee entry; and there, too, were his strong stallions; and his gentle old brood mares. They were all there, all dead, lying with their keen limbs and shapely necks extended on the blood-soaked plain.

But wait! The kaleidoscope of colors before Tilcoax seemed to be blending. The faintest murmur stirred upon the breeze. There appeared to be some life emerging from the lifeless forms. Soon, in the clouds above the bloody river, Tilcoax caught sight of something resplendent in the setting sun. It was of such red brilliance that he raised his arm to protect his eyes from its burning glory. Thus protected, he gazed again. There before him and standing proud in the shadow of the sun was the most magnificent stallion Tilcoax had ever seen, a chestnut son of royalty.

Amotkan spoke, "Do not lose heart, brave Chief Tilcoax. This is a spirit horse formed from the spirits of your beloved riches. One day, he will return with the speed, the endurance, and the pluck of all the horses dead on the battlefield. He will enter into the body of a colt, and will go forth to conquer all the horses of the earth. The losses of your people will be redeemed in his name, Spokane, Child of the Sun."

Slowly, Chief Tilcoax awoke from his sleep. Frantically, he searched the sky, but nothing there remained as evidence of his dream. Yet somehow, he felt refreshed and renewed. He hastened to reassure his warriors that he was all right, and he told them of Amotkan's promise.

The warriors listened, but thought that poor, old Tilcoax had lost his senses, as well as his horses. They were disillusioned, weary of war, and desired only a chance to live peacefully the lives of their fathers. Gently, they lifted Tilcoax onto his blanket and carried him home.

For years, the vision of Chief Tilcoax was a popular tale among the tribal members. However, few believed it bore any truth; that is until the old chief died. Then, as they gathered to perform the burial rituals, they marveled at the unmistakable look of triumph that marked Chief Tilcoax's wise and strangely confident face. □

2 The Wrongs Of Colonel Wright
Facts Behind the Legend

Long ago, in the Spokane Falls and Coeur d'Alene area of the Washington Territory, the Spokane Indians fought for survival in a wilderness land. They fished and farmed. Their farms were not the striped prairies of the white man, but the pleasant, golden meadows tended by Mother Nature herself. Here, the women harvested camass, balsamroot, bitterroot, wild onion, and the wild carrot. They gathered grasses and herbs. From the hills of summer and early fall came the serviceberry, blueberry, wild currant, golden currant, squaw currant, hawthorne, gooseberry, Oregon grape, chokecherry, and the huckleberry. Amotkan, their creator, was good. Ceremonies of thanksgiving were held twice a year.

The wealth of the Spokanes was not to be counted in parcels of land, pouches of gold, or pockets of coins. Wealth was horses. They prized the swift, sleek ones that they raced, and the courage of the sure-footed buffalo horses. Breaking these ponies occupied many hours. Ropes were tied around the animals' bellies to restrain them, and sometimes blindfolds were used. Riding at a full gallop was sport; hair flying and voices flung into the wind. Young braves found vent for their competitive urges by racing their horses against one another while proud elders bet high stakepiles on favorites. Some of these contests had as many as thirty horses racing in heats as long as five miles.

Led by a wise chief named Garry who had attended the trader's school at Lake Winnipeg, Canada, and who was familiar with English, French, the Episcopal faith, and agriculture, the Spokanes were far from being "savages". Chief Garry attempted to instill in his people the value of education. He gathered them together on Sundays to worship in the church he had built. Here, he taught them prayers, hymns, the Ten Commandments, and the rules of right conduct according to the Bible; all this so that they might see God when they died. Children and adults were taught English, agriculture, and Christianity. Garry actively sought to change the ways of tradition — one wife, not three or four, and farming with a plow and hoe, not just the random harvesting of the unpredictable resources of nature. He advocated a peaceful path. It was his contention that the key to the Indian's survival was learning the ways of the white man. Compromise and friendship insured for the Spokanes a portion of their homeland. Diligently, Chief Garry labored to convince the young.

As with each generation, what is prudent is not always what is acceptable. The young felt that Chief Garry was weak. They did not heed his calls for reason. Instead, alarmed by the coming of Colonel Steptoe and his troops, as well as the proposed building of the Mullan Road from Fort Walla Walla to Fort Benton, the decision was made to fight. The white man's group was small; the Spokane were many. With victory, life in the old tradition could continue unchanged, but change was inevitable.

In April of 1858, Lieutenant Colonel E. J. Steptoe began to send reports indicative of brewing trouble. Two of his men had been killed near the Palouse River on their way to Colville. Palouse Indians had raided the Walla Walla Valley and carried off cattle and horses, including thirteen head of cattle belonging to the army. White people living in Colville had asked that troops be sent to protect their lives and property. Steptoe began to look for the Indian "outlaws". He hoped to check their disturbances by peaceful means. He was not equipped for confrontation.

Early on May 6, 1858, in the company of 158 men, Lieutenant Colonel Steptoe crossed Palouse country and headed for the Spokane lands. Despite warnings that native resistance would be made, Steptoe continued onward.

On Sunday morning, May 16, aware that a force of Indians was assembling somewhere ahead, Steptoe advanced. Suddenly 600 to 1,200 Spokane, Coeur d'Alene, Palouse, and Flathead Indians appeared. They were well-mounted and armed with rifles. The two forces halted a hundred yards apart, and several Spokanes came forward. They repeated their intent to fight any further advance, and though they professed the belief that Steptoe came in peace, they would not allow him to cross the Spokane River. Steptoe realized that confrontation was unavoidable. He began a retreat, postponing the battle as long as possible

On May 17, Father Joseph Joset of the Coeur d'Alene mission sought to defuse the situation and arranged for Chief Vincent of the Coeur d'Alenes to visit with Steptoe. Though Vincent seemed to believe Steptoe's professed peaceful intentions, he was interrupted in his counsel by news of trouble beginning in the rear of the march. Promptly, he returned to his tribesmen.

The conflict began. Each side fought for favorable positions. Battle came as a series of short charges and retreats. Much signaling was going on, and the Indians were apparently receiving reinforcements. The army, on the other hand, had little hope of attaining aid. The distance to Fort Walla Walla was too great, and though a Nez Perce scout had been dispatched the previous evening, there was little chance of his getting through. The decision made, a final stand was contemplated on a nearby eminence.

So far, the army's toll was relatively light. Two officers, Captain Taylor and Lieutenant Gaston, and five others of Steptoe's command were dead. Six were badly wounded, seven less seriously so, and one was missing. In addition, three of their Indian allies were dead. The tribes' losses were heavier. At least nine braves were killed and forty or fifty were wounded.

The Steptoe decision to take to the hill appeared to give the Indians confidence. They at once surrounded the area and began to ascend the slopes. Many camouflaged their movements by tying grass to their heads. At nightfall, they ceased their advance, eagerly awaiting their daylight victory on the morrow.

Tomorrow held promise, but it was a promise which couldn't be kept. The command hastened in the dead of night for safety beyond the Snake River, ninety miles away. Dead were buried. Wounded were lashed in their saddles. Horses of light color were blanketed to sustain the cover of darkness. Extra animals were left picketed on the hill. Supplies were abandoned. Division of this booty, the extra animals and the supplies, delayed the tribes in their pursuit. It was a wise and calculated act.

When news of Steptoe's defeat reached the nation's capitol, much was made of it. Support was garnered to crush the offenders with a strong hand.

In Indian camps, the news was cause for celebration. Young braves danced, raced horses, and bragged of their victory. Beneath it all, wiser and older braves harbored disquiet in their hearts. They sensed in this battle not an end, but rather the beginning of an end.

By June 23, 1858, General Newman S. Clarke had arrived at Fort Vancouver, and he vigorously began preparing troops for war with the Indians. The latter, after being informed by Father Joset and Father Congiato, S. J., of the intensity of the planned army reprisal, ceased their chants and dances of war and began cautiously to seek a peaceful settlement.

Declaring that troops would pass through Indian country whenever he pleased to send them and that the road to Fort Benton would be built, General Clarke ordered the return of all stolen property and the immediate surrender of all the hostiles who had fired on the troops. Returning the stolen property, especially the horses, was impossible.

They were irretrievably lost in a complex maze of trading from person to person. As for surrendering the perpetrators, this too was an unachievable task. In a system of government where numerous chiefs exercised limited control, no one Indian had the power to enforce Clarke's ultimatums. Thus, the making of peace, based upon these terms, was an unattainable goal from the Indians' point of view.

General Clarke was not unaware of the hopelessness of his request. Clarke was already preparing to strike the enemy. On July 4, 1858, he ordered Colonel George Wright into the field. Wright had in his command 570 regulars of whom 190 were in four troops of dragoons and 380 were infantry, or artillery serving as infantry. In addition to the regulars, there were thirty Nez Perces and 100 packers and other employees. Rations for thirty-eight days, ammunition, and other supplies necessitated two pack trains, and about 800 animals, including the mounts and 400 mules.

On August 3, 1858, Spokane Chief Garry sent word with Father Congiato to General Clarke. He spoke of his regret over the recent "useless" fight which Steptoe had begun, and his people had finished, despite his advice to the contrary. Cleverly, Garry omitted mention of Clarke's demands and expressed hope for a future of peace.

At the same time, Spokane Chief Polatkin also spoke. He attempted to explain the Indian's method of concluding wars: "[We] bury the dead [including the exchanging of properties] and talk and live on good terms. [We] don't speak of more blood."

But more blood was to be. The Indians did not cease their opposition to the invasion of their homeland, and General Clarke continued to assert the rights of the United States in this matter pertinent to the benefit and safety of the American people. For him, the impending war was just punishment for previous crimes. It was his duty to put down the Indian uprising. As a soldier, it was simple obedience to a higher command.

The first confrontation between Wright and the Indians occurred on September 1, 1858. It was called the Battle of the Four Lakes, and it was a victory for the army. Indian losses were heavy.

At the Battle of the Spokane Plains on September 5, 1858, Spotted Coyote, a Pend 'Orielle chief, stated: "There is no use of our fighting. We can do nothing against cannon. The whites are far superior to us in their arms. We must give up fighting and make peace, or leave the country." This view was shared by his fellow warriors by the end of the day.

Spokane Chief Garry met with Wright on September 7, after having been chosen peacemaker because of his white man's speech and manner of dress. Garry attempted to explain his lack of control over the warring faction of his tribe and to create a feeling of sympathetic

Left — Chief Garry of the Spokanes. Sought peaceful solutions to the problems created by the white immigration. Right — Colonel Wright, the perpetrator of the horse massacre in Washington State in 1858. Spokane Public Library photos.

understanding for his position. This feeling could then be used as a stepping stone to peace.

Wright chose to ignore Garry's conciliatory tone and took this opportunity to demand unconditional surrender and to threaten extermination. He said: "I have met you in two bloody battles; you have been badly whipped; you have lost several chiefs and many warriors killed or wounded. I have not lost a man or animal; I have a large force, and you Spokanes, Coeur d'Alenes, Palouses, and Pend 'Oreilles may unite, and I can defeat you as badly as before. I did not come into this country to ask you to make peace; I come here to fight. Now when you are tired of war, and ask for peace, I will tell you what you must do: You must come to me with your arms, with your women and children, and everything you have, and lay them at my feet; you must put your faith in me and trust to my mercy. If you do this, I shall then dictate the terms upon which I will grant you peace. If you do not do this, war will be made on you this year and next and until your nation shall be exterminated."

Once more, the terms of peace were outside the realms of possibility. Across the cultural gap between the two races, no bridge could be built.

A series of atrocities followed. Some, not surprisingly, were left out of the military reports. One Indian was hung after a brief "trial."

Another, Amtoola, an interpreter with some knowledge of English, came seeking a conference with Colonel Wright. Swimming the Spokane River on horseback and carrying a white flag, he cautiously approached. The soldiers shot him dead.

September 8, the Indians attempted to drive their stock south. The soldiers dismounted and followed them into the hills. There they dispersed the Indian herders at Liberty Lake, also known in some accounts as Wyatt Lake. After making two attempts to capture natives' cattle and finding them too wild, Wright's men succeeded in rounding up about 800 horses. Most of these animals were reported to belong to Chief Tilcoax of the Palouse Tribe.

Watching from the hills, the Indians witnessed the driving off of their horses. They were not alarmed. These valued possessions could be recaptured; circumstances governing the army's march commanded their release.

Horses were the survival gear of the frontier. To the Indians, they were a symbol of affluence. Horses meant life and sustenance. The killing of horses was considered a heinous crime, but this was a time of war. Normal rules did not apply. Wright concluded that without horses the Indians were powerless. The destruction of the horses was seen as a justifiable means to end the Indian resistance. It was viewed as practical since it would be impossible to control the herd during an eastward march. The enemy would try to stampede them, they were wild, and they created a dangerous risk for the command's animals as well.

Thus, on September 9, the soldiers built a log corral, and then, one by one lassoed the horses and took them from the corral to the banks of the Spokane River, near the site of the present-day Spokane Bridge. Here, at what later would be referred to as Wright's Bone Yard, they methodically shot the older horses. Colts, they knocked in the head. Brood mares neighed frantically into the night; their sounds haunting the soldiers and bringing many to tears.

The morning of September 10, it was decided to speed up the operation. Two companies of soldiers were lined up on the banks of the Spokane River. They fired volleys into the corral and were later aided by two more companies until the awesome and gruesome total of 690 horses had been killed — 130 being saved for use by the expedition.

One soldier, Keyes, later wrote: "It was a cruel sight to see so many noble beasts shot down... in their beautiful faces an appeal for mercy."

Another view by Henry L. Weinrush is simply told to Indian children: "The soldiers probably liked horses just as we do today, but soldiers learn to obey. They killed the ponies: every appaloosa, roan, gray, sorrel, bay, black, pinto, and chestnut."

Later, Mr. Weinrush writes of the significance of this loss to the tribes.

"Their ponies were all dead. Without ponies, the Indians could not go to the fishing sites. They could not go to the mountains after their huckleberries. Indians could not ride to places where they could hunt deer. They could not ride to Montana to trade for buffalo meat and robes. During the next winter, many of the Indians were very hungry and cold. When the soldiers burned the food, they also burned teepees and blankets and fur robes. Chief Garry wept when he saw what had happened to his people."

Colonel Wright concluded his campaign by signing treaties with the Coeur d'Alenes and the Spokanes on September 17, and 22, respectively. He returned to Fort Walla Walla on October 5. Later, he served during the Civil War as a brigadier general in charge of volunteers along the Pacific Coast. In 1865, Wright was to assume command of the Department of the Columbia, but he drowned off the coast of northern California in the wreck of the steamer, Brother Jonathan.

A man of peace, Chief Garry, felt it easier to move than to resist. He left his Pleasant Prairie Farm and later his home beside the river in Peaceful Valley. His wife and daughter found work among the white households of Spokane, and small white children played on cliffs above the old chief's tattered teepee — tormenting him by rolling rocks onto his home below. Garry did not get angry with them, but was instead deeply saddened by their lack of respect and understanding. Once a proud chief, noble and wise, Garry died in Indian Canyon in 1892 — a lonely, old man estranged in the land of his birth.

The capture and destruction of the horses effectively put an end to the Indian uprising. Its effect was a crushing blow to their way of life. Their spirits were broken. It should come as no wonder then that from this devastating tragedy, Spokane's legend of hope and triumph grew. □

3 The Armstrong Connection

It is an unusual transition, from the Wright Campaign of 1858 and the Indian vision of a "super" horse to the life of Montana mining speculator, Noah Armstrong. However, persistence and patience will bring order to the present and peace with the past, for Noah Armstrong became the owner of a very special racehorse named Spokane.

Noah Armstrong was born in Kingston, Ontario, Canada in January of 1823. He later homesteaded near Lehilier, Minnesota. His wife, Hannah Howd, was born in January of 1822 at Camden, New York. They had three children: Emma, born in May, 1856; Charles, born in February, 1858; and Ida, born in August, 1860. Ida died at the age of four in Lehilier.

In 1873, Noah, a pharmacist and chemist as well as promoter extraordinaire, moved to Montana Territory. Mining records of the time show that on September 4 of that year, Noah Armstrong and his partner, Benjamin Harvey, staked the following lodes: the Utopia Lode, the Monoa Lode, the Symington Lode, and the Vitalis Lode. On September 5, they claimed the Cleve Lode, the Avon Lode, the Atlantis Lode, and the Alta Lode. On the 19th of September, they added the Saxon Lode to their holdings, and on September 25, the Hecla Lode. This last became a source of personal wealth for Armstrong, its riches purchasing fame for a fledgling state.

In 1875, with another partner, Charles F. Dahler, Noah organized and built a smelter at Glendale, Beaverhead County, Montana Territory. Glendale was so named by happenstance. A chip of wood, on which was penned Clinton on one side and Glendale on the other, was tossed over the assay office wall. It landed Glendale side up.

By influencing Eastern interests, Armstrong was able to form the Hecla Consolidated Mining Company with headquarters in Indianapolis. The

Noah Armstrong, the owner of Spokane. Armstrong family photo.

mining claims involved in this transaction included the Cleve, Avon, Alta, Atlantis, Hecla, Cleopatra, Ariadne, Mark Anthony, and the Trapper. The Company's business was defined as the mining of gold, silver, copper, lead, and other metals and minerals, and the smelting of those ores. The assets of the Company were appraised at $1,500,000. Noah Armstrong and Elias C. Atkins were the primary stockholders. Both owned 2,323 shares worth $116,150.

Census figures of Glendale taken in 1880 and 1890 show populations of 678 and 1111 respectively. This was a thriving community, and Noah Armstrong was its founder. By 1876, Armstrong and his business associates controlled the mines, the smelter, the only bank, two general merchandise outlets, and the post office.

Until 1879, Noah managed the Hecla Company. During his tenure, the mines produced 1,000,000 ounces of silver annually as well as thousands of tons of lead and copper.

One account of the period taken from the book, *Not In Precious Metals Alone: Manuscript History of Montana,* quotes Alma Coffin, who along with her two sisters left St. Paul, Minnesota, in 1878 to join their father in Glendale. They traveled first by steamboat down the Mississippi River and then up the Missouri River as far as Fort Benton, Montana. The last leg of their journey was a jouncing thirty-two hour stagecoach ride. Here is what Alma wrote on August 7, 1878: "...We were allowed only 25 pounds [of baggage] on the stage, so we worked half the night unpacking and repacking, and trying to decide what articles to take and what to leave in the trunks. The trunks are to be forwarded by ox freight, and we will not see them again until mid-winter...[In the stage] There were two seats inside facing each other with room for three on each seat. The coach springs were not very good or perhaps too good for one's head sometimes bumped against the top...The roads were bad in many places. The passengers climbed down and out helping to pry out the wheels. Once when we offered to walk, the driver called cheerily, 'Sit still, ladies. Sit still, and we'll all be buried together...' Mud splashed us the first part of the journey and dust covered us the last part...I know why people love the West. Its beauty and grandeur [is] made of mountains, rocks, and trees, and canyons, and dashing streams. The vast landscapes revealed in the clear atmosphere [are] beyond all description. The people are friendly and hospitable. Newcomers are warmly greeted for they bring news from the states."

Later, on September 1, 1879, Alma penned:

"Glendale, the mining camp in which our father lived and the destination of our long journey of the month is located on the northeastern [edge] of Beaverhead County on Trapper Creek, a small branch which flows into the Big Hole River. At Glendale are located many of the buildings of the Hecla Mining Company including the smelter, a large

Left — Noah Armstrong, family portrait by Emma Armstrong. Emma was an artist and the daughter of Noah. Right — Hannah Howd Armstrong, family portrait by Emma Armstrong.

roaster, assay office, warehouse, blacksmith shop, sack house, iron house, powder houses, coal sheds, stables, and dwellings for the officials. The Hecla Hospital, a clean, up-to-date institution is also located here in this seemingly out-of-the-way place. Glendale has one main street winding up the gulch and a number of little farm houses and log cabins scattered along the stony hillside. The only vegetation is the prickly pear cactus and a scant growth of low bushes excepting the willows on the creek, which tumbles down to the bottom of the narrow gulch. The smelter gives employment to the community and reduces the copper and silver ore brought down by freight wagons from the Trapper Mountain mines nine miles above. There are more than a hundred working men about the town. Those who have families in the states expect to either send for them or return home. The young men are usually bustling, ambitious fellows eager to make a stake. 'I'm not in the mountains for my health' is a common expression frequently heard. Some are well-educated and from good families back East. Good substantial working clothes and non-conventional manners are the rule. There are, of course, large tenders of men known to be gamblers, but these are not perceived by the better class of citizens' moral standards [to be of] smooth address and good appearance. Besides ourselves, there are three young ladies here. Miss Armstrong from Minnesota is visiting her father,

The Glendale Smelter in the 1880's. Glendale, Montana. Ben Goody collection.

two girls of fifteen are reported to be engaged to middle-aged men, and a but-little-older newcomer is receiving much attention and is quite giddy in consequence. Dancing and card playing are the chief amusements. A little Sunday school is maintained, and church services are held once or twice a month by Reverend W. W. Van Orsdel or Reverend Duncan; both of the ministers [are] of the Methodist Episcopal Church. Bishop Tuttle visits and conducts a service in each once a year. Father taught the Glendale school last winter, and he often laughs of the only stipulation by the trustees, 'The teacher must not get drunk in school hours,' and in this instance, the teacher had always been a total abstainer. Gossip is ripe, as in most small places, and everyone's affairs are either known or guessed. Characters [are] quickly read, and people [are] rated at their worth. Prices are high and change smaller than two bits is not usually considered."

Glendale was The West. On June 16, 1884, Jacob Miller, a pharmacist, wrote to his fiancee in Kansas:

"The store has been crowded with customers and loafers all evening. Our place is headquarters for everybody. We keep besides drugs, a big stock of potions, fishing tackle, sporting goods, all sorts of glassware and fresh fruit. Fruit gives me a great deal of work. We receive fresh fruit every morning from Ogden, Utah. All kinds, strawberries, peaches, plums, apricots, pears, lemons, and oranges, and I tell you it's quite a

 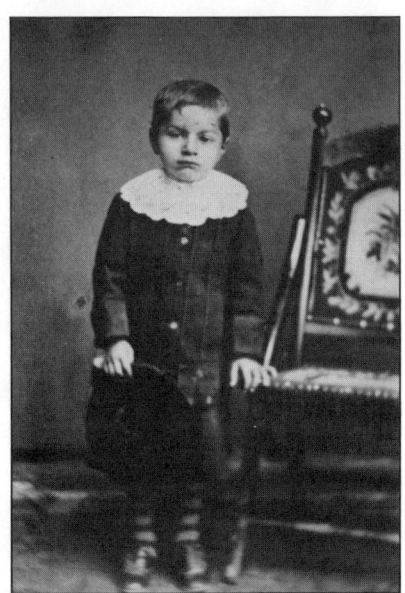

Left — Emma Armstrong, Hardy and Embury photographers, Faribault, Minnesota. Right — Harry Armstrong, son of Charles and Elizabeth Armstrong, grandson of Noah Armstrong. Died of diphtheria in Glendale, Montana, July, 1883. Armstrong family photos.

job to take care of it when you've got a lot of other work to do besides... There has been a great deal of excitement in the camp since yesterday. At four o'clock yesterday afternoon, they had a horse race. At seven o'clock, they had a foot race. The men passed right by the store. This morning at ten, they had a wrestling match and this evening at five another horse race. Everything is excitement here, and everybody goes in for enjoyment of a coarse and rough nature. The majority of people around here seem to think that a saloon is the next best thing to paradise and that foot races, dog fights, horse races, etc. are the only subjects fit to talk about."

In April of 1886, Noah Armstrong, in cooperation with his son-in-law, C. W. Turner, and a railroad promoter, S. S. Glidden, contemplated the building of a railroad to the mines. This was eventually completed and sold to the Northern Pacific Railroad Company.

Glendale did boast some class. It had an opera house for traveling theatrical troops and the largest roller skating rink in the Northwest. It also possessed a track for horse racing, and one church.

In this church, Noah Armstrong's children were married. Charles married Elizabeth Mannheim on Christmas Day in 1878. The Reverend Shippen officiated. Emma married Charles W. Turner on September 11, 1879, in a ceremony conducted by Bishop Tuttle.

Left — Noah Armstrong's wife, Hannah. Right — Charles Armstrong, son of Noah and Hannah Armstrong. Armstrong family photos.

In Glendale, too, the Armstrong grandchildren were born and baptized. Emma had two sons, Armstrong and Charles W., Jr. Charles and Elizabeth gave life to four of their eight children in Glendale. There was Harry, born in November, 1879; Nellie, born in May, 1881; Ethel, born in December, 1882; and Carl, born in November, 1884. Of these last, only one survived the hardships of living in the mining camp.

When the demand for silver died in 1892, Glendale died too. Today, with an imagination nurtured by a romantic nature, Glendale remains much the same. It rests at an elevation of approximately one mile and is located about four miles from Melrose, Montana. Melrose is just off Interstate 15, south of Butte. There is still plenty of prickly pear and bunch grass covering the surrounding hillsides. Ancient willow trees woefully shade the bubbling Trapper Creek. Main Street threads its way past skeletal remains as it proceeds up the mountain to Greenwood, Lion City, Hecla, and eventually, the 11,000-foot massive face of Lion Mountain, some twelve miles further on. There is the smokestack, only the base of which is original. The rest was burned in a fire in 1879. This stark landmark stands as a lone sentinel, watching over this abandoned Montana treasure chest. Also visible is the site of the Methodist Episcopal Church, the framework of the assay office, the foundation of the Hecla Mercantile, and the shell of the wooden schoolhouse, which first served as the Hecla Mining Offices. Still in livable condition is the Doctor's stone house, possibly the location of the twelve-bed Hecla Hospital. Abundant is slag rock, lying black and lead-laden along the steep slopes leading to the creek. Here, too, are square nails; the symbols of construction from times long ago.

Life in Glendale was not easy. A quiet stroll through the cemetery reveals the reality of frontier times. The often marble headstones, as well as footstones, bear a sad tale of lost youth. The Armstrong family plot is enclosed within a wrought iron fence which boasts ornate posts that bear flower urns at their tops. Here are the graves of three of Noah's grandchildren: Harry, Nellie, and Ethel; ages 3, 2, and 1 respectively. All died from an epidemic of diptheria in the year 1883. Also buried here is Hannah Howd Armstrong, Noah's wife, who passed away on June 4, 1885. An elegant marble memorial marks her grave. Once standing four feet in height, it was broken in half by a herd of wandering cattle.

Another cause of death in Glendale besides disease was a natural disaster, snowslides. These occurred quite frequently, usually in the spring, some as late as May. Taking many lives as they cascaded down the steep mountainside, snowslides crushed cabins and buried the occupants.

Gazing upon this silent testimony of the past, one cannot help but feel that those buried here are the ultimate victors. For all time, they possess a lovely, high and secluded hill with a clear and panoramic view of the majestic Pioneer Mountains, peacefully resting in a rugged land.

Noah Armstrong survived Glendale though he lost a part of himself forever on her hillside. He entrusted his mining claims to the care of his son-in-law and business associates, descendants of whom continue to own stock in the Hecla Consolidated Mining Company of today. Noah went in search of a less stressful enterprise. He settled upon the raising and racing of Thoroughbred horses. A hobby that he had long enjoyed became his profession. This decisive career change brought joy from depression, success from calamity, and fame to Montana and the entire Pacific Northwest. □

4 The Round Barn

Nestled at the foot of the Ruby Mountains, one and one-half miles north of Twin Bridges, Montana, there is a huge, round barn three stories tall. It is a magnificent remnant of a gallant age, from its awesome dimensions to its grand entryway complete with a four-by-eight foot, hand-carved reproduction of Rosa Bonheur's "Horse Fair." Today, though weathered and worn from years of neglect and exposure to the elements, the picture is still visible. Completed by Emma Armstrong, Noah's daughter, it speaks well of the education and culture that was brought by the citizens of the Montana Territory to this wild land of frontier dreams. In 1986, Marla Edmiston's watercolor of the barn won placement in the Great Falls State Fair Permanent Collection. The round barn today serves as a local curiosity. Once, a tour bus pulled up to the entrance and unloaded its occupants, sure that a guide would be present to describe this unusual piece of architecture and boast of its history. Though there was not then any official recognition of this structure, it does have a significant story to tell. For here, in 1886, Spokane, Thoroughbred of excellence, subject of legend, Child of the Sun, and Spirit Horse, was born. This chestnut stallion is what makes the site famous, for it is the birthplace of Montana's only Kentucky Derby winner.

John Mannheim, the father-in-law of Noah Armstrong's son, bequeathed his Jefferson Valley ranch to his wife, Veronica, on the occasion of his death in 1879. Veronica in turn left the ranch to Elizabeth, Charles Armstrong's wife, in 1882. Noah then purchased the property for $5,000. In 1884, Noah acquired an additional section of the Mannheim estate from the appraiser, Jacob Wyrouch, for the consideration of $15. Noah determined to build his horse farm on the site, giving it the name Doncaster Ranch in honor of one of his favorite horses. Noah believed strongly in the theory that the mountain altitude and wild bunch grass of Montana would provide an ideal environment for the raising of fast, strong, hardy, healthy, and superior race horses. These horses would possess the necessary stamina to survive life in an often inhospitable land as well as to win on a race track. Moving to the area, Noah established a pharmacy and general merchandise store in Twin Bridges. This enterprise, as well as his mining successes, provided Noah Armstrong with adequate funds to finance his elaborate barn and breeding operation.

In a previously unpublished paper penned for Noah Armstrong's son, Charles, the ranch is described as follows:

"Doncaster Ranch, Madison County, Montana, the property of Charles Armstrong, Esq. is — throughout the northwest, at least — celebrated as being the birthplace of several of the most famous race horses of recent years. The horses which first saw the light of day upon its domain, and which have won name and fame upon the running and trotting tracks of the United States, can be counted by the score, and the most noted of them have even attained a reputation for speed and power of endurance which has extended wherever these attributes in the equine race find recognition and encouragement. Few, indeed, are the followers of turf events throughout the racing world who have not heard of and marveled at the great performances of the splendid 'Spokane,' who was foaled here in 1886, and whose famous victories in 1888, and 1889 crowned him the King of the Turf. To all such people, Doncaster Ranch will be regarded as a place of historic interest. The site is beyond compare, one of the most favorable localities for fashionable horse breeding purposes that is to be found in all the famous inter-mountain region. It is beautifully situated in the picturesque valley of the Jefferson River, and embraces within its limits something over four thousand acres of land lying along and adjacent to the noble river of that name. To be accurate, the owner can read his title clear to four thousand and eighty acres (if we may be permitted use of a trite westernism), the 'best-land-that-lies out o'doors.' Its soil is a deeply, alluvial loam, the accumulation of many generations of wash from the neighboring foothills, and it is of remarkable fertility. In its native condition, it bears a prolific growth of the rich and nutritious grasses which have made Montana so famous as a pasturage and feeding ground for horses and stock cattle of every kind. Under cultivation, the various imported grasses — such as timothy, red-top, blue grass, lucerue, and the different varieties of clover — are produced in such profuse abundance on its rich meadow lands that the statement of their yield would be received with incredulity by many who have not actually witnessed the results obtained from successively recurring hay harvests. These, however, have emphatically and indubitably proven the great fecundity of the region hereabouts in this respect.

"Nor is the soil peculiarly strong in its capacity for the prolific

"Horse Fair" by Rosa Bonheur. A likeness of this was carved over the entrance to the round barn by Emma Armstrong. The Metropolitan Museum of Art, New York City, New York. Gift of Cornelius Vanderbilt, 1887.

production of annual food vegetation alone. The experience of many years of successful agricultural tillage has given the most ample demonstration of the fact that it possesses the necessary qualities to produce all the cereals in quantities not exceeded by the most favored grain-growing regions in the state, while the uniform success which has rewarded the numerous 'market gardeners' in the neighborhood, ever since the settlement of the valley, some thirty years ago, furnishes complete and sufficient evidence that almost every variety of table vegetable can be raised here with most profitable results. The necessities of the region have not required much tree planting, but what little has been done in this line has shown that, when the occasion demands it, horticulture can also be advantageously added to the number of rural pursuits. Under the eminently favorable conditions of soil and climate in the great basin of which the Jefferson Valley forms a part, not only do all kinds of vegetation yield in surpassing abundance, but the almost unbroken immunity from killing frosts during the growing season insures a most excellent quality in the crops when they are garnered. As matter of well established meteorological record, the Jefferson Valley is noted throughout the state for the mild salubrity of its climate and the uniformly equable temperature which marks the seasons in their annual recurrence.

"So patent were its advantages, from an agricultural point of view that, when the discovery of immense deposits of gold in Bannack, Alder Gulch, and other mountain regions surrounding the great basin drew thousands of adventurers into the then trackless wilderness in search of the yellow metal, the country about the Jefferson River was the first to attract the attention of the farming portion of that immigration, and on Doncaster Ranch and in its neighborhood were located first farms by the pioneer husbandmen of the embryo State of Montana. The success which attended these farmers was phenomenal. The statement is supported by abundant corroborative testimony that crops from seventy to ninety bushels of barley were not at all of uncommon occurrence, wheat yielding from fifty to seventy bushels, and oats frequently exceeding one hundred bushels to the acre. Add to this the fact that many neighbors of Doncaster Ranch have become wealthy by the cultivation of corn, tomatoes, melons, and the several varieties of table vegetables during more than a quarter of a century, and are still remuneratively engaged in the business, and sufficient attestation is had of all that has been said of the adaptability of this region for producing all kinds of vegetation that are cultivable in the temperate zone.

"During the decade of the 70's, when the decline of placer gold mining industry caused an exodus of the major portion of the mining population, the resultant loss of market had a correspondingly depressing effect upon other branches of the business, and agricultural pursuits were not exempted from the effects of the general commercial stagnation which followed. The great mining camp of Butte, which lies about thirty miles northwest from the ranch was as yet in an embryonic condition, and few even of the most enthusiastic, had any idea of the wondrous proportions which she was destined to attain within the next few years. The first log cabin had not yet been erected in the great 'Smelter City' of Anaconda. The mammoth mine of that name, which now supplies the mills and smelters with hundreds of car-loads of copper ore per day was an undeveloped prospect hole, and there was little to indicate that an industrious, thriving population of thirty or forty thousand souls were soon to establish their homes and habitations in the near vicinity of the valley. The consequence of these conditions was an inevitable and natural one. The raising of grain, upon the extensive scale which had been the custom, ceased to be remunerative to the husbandman. It was, therefore, necessarily discontinued, and production limited to conform to the inflexible law of supply and demand. Farmers found their occupation gone, or at least, unprofitable, and, in many instances vacated their holdings, and drifted with the adventurous tide. The lands in the Jefferson Valley, on account of their remoteness from what little was left of the great mining towns, were notwithstanding their great fertility, among the first to be abandoned. If wonder was expressed why so many fine farms upon which thousands of dollars had been expended in improvements, were ruthlessly, if reluctantly, given up, it was met by the clinching argument and unanswerable question: 'What is the use of farming if you cannot sell your crops?' To this the interrogator could only respond, 'What indeed.'

"It was during this period that Mr. Noah Armstrong, father of the present proprietor of Doncaster Ranch, and at that time general manager and Superintendent of the Hecla Consolidated Mining Company of Glendale, became interested in the matter of breeding and raising fine horses, a pursuit for which he had a natural affinity. He foresaw, with that sagacity and prescience which were among his distinguishing characteristics, that the time was approaching when there would be a constantly increasing and popular demand for a better class of horseflesh than was common to the Territory in those days. To supply this demand, and to fill this long felt want became one of his chief ambitions. Being a man with whom to think was to act, he was not long in getting to work on plans for the consummation of his project. After careful study and much consideration, he became firmly of the opinion (the correctness of which has been fully demonstrated by ensuing results) that the conditions existing in Montana were eminently favorable for the rearing, in superior form, of representatives of the most distinguished and fashionable equine families. His observations extended through several years of personal and patient investigation convinced him that in point of climate, soil, pasturage, and the other natural accessories to his purpose, Montana was the equal, if not the superior, of the best known horse-raising districts of the United States not excepting even the highly extolled 'blue-grass region' of Kentucky. The experience of others in a similar, though less ambitious direction strongly fortified his estimate of the correctness of his judgment, and he determined to go into the business on a scale which would insure a brilliant triumph if successful, but great financial loss should failure attend the enterprise. The first important thing to be done was to find a suitable location. For this purpose, he made many journeys to several parts of the (at that time) Territory, but nowhere could he find a place which impressed him so favorably with its desirability as the farming region of the upper Jefferson Valley described earlier. Here was par excellence, the ideal location for the carrying out of his conception, and here he determined to establish the farm. By location, purchase, and the expenditure of many thousands of dollars, he founded a horse- breeding establishment which in magnitude and superiority of equipment is not excelled between the Mississippi River and the Pacific Coast.

"It was a daring venture, but the success which has been achieved has proven that Mr. Armstrong was in no wise at fault in his estimates of the feasibility of his scheme. From its inception, the details of the management of Doncaster Ranch have been followed with the strict adherence to its founder's predominant idea that the introduction and cultivation of the finest and purest strains of horse blood, intelligently and honestly pursued would be a profitable investment, and the results have far exceeded the anticipations. With this as the prime mover in the enterprise, the stocking of the ranch was begun by importing

The Doncaster Ranch of Noah Armstrong near Twin Bridges, Montana, as it appeared in the late 1880s. Byron Bayers collection.

representatives of the most notable running and trotting horse families in the country. To these, only such others were added as were proven by blood and birth to be of indisputable pedigree and uncontestable merit, and by faithfully pursuing the method thus established, the stables of Doncaster Ranch have become noted all over the country for the number and superior racing qualities of their product, of both trotters and thoroughbreds."

The author then gives the details of some of the "horse fathers" of the ranch. Included in this list is Tom Bowling, a son of the "never-to-be-forgotten, Lexington" and the noble mare, Lucy Fowler. Tom Bowling, a bay stallion, was purchased by Armstrong in March of 1884. Tom Bowling is described in one publication as being a "picture horse"; nothing was more beautiful on the course. He could go on and on and beat the best horses of his era over the longest courses of his time. His triumphs, it is said, were won in a lordly way. Tom Bowling, though an acknowledged great on the track, was a demon in his stall. He was obsessed by a hatred for rats and would stand all day watching for a chance to pounce on one in his box and stamp it to death. He was a man-killer, as well as a rat-killer. Having killed one man and seriously injured scores of others, he kept everyone around him terrorized. It took several men to lead him out for service and everybody was cautioned to keep at a safe distance when the old stallion appeared, dragging two or three grooms and their helpers along after him. Tom Bowling reared, turned, and lunged while bellowing like a bull—truly an exhibition meant to incur both fear and respect.

In 1872, as a youngster of two, Tom was "Colt of the Year." At three, he won eight of nine races, including the $5,500 Jerome Stakes at Jerome Park in New York on October 4, 1873. As a four-year-old, Tom was unbeaten, winning the Travers Stakes at Saratoga "by thirty yards." This feat was accomplished by beating another great of this era, Springbok, the winner of the Belmont Stakes. The fact that Tom Bowling stood at the Doncaster Ranch is testament to Noah's determination to obtain the best.

The ranch itself was named for another stallion of Noah's, Doncaster, a splendid black, 16 hands high. Doncaster was a trotter of fine blood and notable record.

Other fine horses attributed to this Montana ranch include Grey Cloud, full brother to Spokane, who had brilliant success as a two-year-old, and as a three-year-old, in 1885, put twenty-eight prizes in his owner's pocket; Monarch, winner of the Viley Stakes, Kentucky Stallion Stakes, and Dixie Stakes in 1881, doing a 3/4 mile at Saratoga in 1:14; Hermine; Lavine, half-sister to Spokane; Montana Maid; Anna Wilkes; Thorn Boy; Montana Regent; Sue Hayden; Barbour's Florida; Lord Raglan, third-place finisher in the 1883 Kentucky Derby; and Montana Wilkes. Such greats as these were identified by individual brass nameplates that detailed their track triumphs and records. These horses represented many thousands of dollars in cash value and were in direct lineage with the most noble horse ancestry in the country.

As the chronicler of the ranch wrote, "No racing stud farm in the northwest can exhibit a grander record of splendid results achieved.

"No provision for their [the horses] well-being and comfort is lacking. The buildings are convenient and substantial. The sanitary condition of the barns and stables has been the subject of due consideration and constant attention, and the employees of the place are chosen with primary regard to their intelligence and perfect familiarity with the routine of duties which they are expected to perform.

"A notable feature of the equipment of the ranch is the magnificent circular barn, which was constructed and fashioned after an original design of Mr. Armstrong's. This structure is so novel in its conception, so convenient in its economy, and withal so admirably adapted to the purpose of its creation that a description of it cannot but be of interest.

"The barn, which may truly be called a model of architectural beauty and convenience, is circular in form and three stories high. The inside diameter of the lower floor is one hundred feet, of the second floor, seventy-six feet, and of the third floor, thirty-six feet. It stands upon stone abutments which are built from piles driven some twelve or fifteen feet below water level to the bedrock beneath. In the construction of these abutments, twelve cords of stone, quarried from the neighboring 'Hell's Canyon' were used. The walls of the barn are formed by three thicknesses of plank, each layer being sandwiched with double sheets of building paper, an arrangement which secures complete warmth in the interior during the most severe weather. The roofing of each story is of similar material, and coated thickly with fire-proof mineral paint. The outer tier of apartments on the ground floor comprise the large box stalls for the horses, the offices, and the dormitories of the employees, the commodious offices being at the left of the entrance, and the sleeping rooms to the right. The stalls are twelve feet square, the division between each being of plank to the height of about four feet, and from thence to the ceiling they are railing, giving each horse a chance to see his neighbors for about halfway around the building. It is claimed that this promotion of neighborly companionship greatly relieves the monotony of indoor horse life, and is very beneficial to the animals which are so kept. The stalls open inward to a track, or a drive-way, twenty-feet wide, which extends all around the building. This is utilized for the handling, breaking, and exercising of the young colts, as well as, the driving of the horses during stormy weather. It also affords ingress to the grain and hay elevators, the entrance being so large that a ten-horse wagon, laden with hay, can easily be driven into the interior of the barn. The drive-way can also be made available, in severe weather for the sheltering of loose stock. It will afford room for three hundred head of horses, without crowding, whenever such an exigency arises. On the inner side of the track is another circular structure. This contains the harness closets, two commodious hospital stalls, the hay and grain elevator, the spiral stairway to the upper floors, and the well-pipe which runs up through the center. In the middle of this structure is the well, which has been sunk to the bedrock, twelve feet below water level, and affords a plentiful supply of water for all purposes.

"The second story contains the granary and the hay-lofts. The latter are arranged next to the outer walls of this story, while the grain bins occupy a large circular room around the well tube. At the time [of this writing], fifty tons of hay were stored in the lofts, and they had an apparent capacity for receiving as much more. The grain bins will hold about twelve thousand bushels of corn. The granary floors slope toward the outside of the apartment. This is for convenience in drawing off the supply for the stables, which is conveyed by automatic appliances to the mangers in the box stalls below.

"The third, and the topmost story holds the water reservoir. It consists of a large circular tank, the storage capacity of which is eleven thousand gallons. The supply is obtained from the well in the center and is elevated to the reservoir by a windmill which surmounts the tower at the top of the building. The stables are supplied from hydrants placed at convenient points on the lower floor, whence the water is conveyed through troughs to the animals in the stalls. The precautions against fire have not been omitted, and each hydrant is fitted with hose by which water can be carried to any part of the building in case of necessity arising from any cause.

"The main building is forty-eight feet high from the ground to the ceiling of the third story, which is surmounted by a tower twelve feet high, the windmill crowning the whole. The height over all is about seventy feet. One hundred and ten thousand feet of lumber were consumed in the construction of the barn; but this only represents a very small figure in the sum total of the expense incurred in its construction. On this point, Mr. Armstrong maintained a modest reserve, which was impenetrable to the writer. But, whatever the cost may have been a triumph has certainly been achieved. In the entire building while every foot of space seems to have its appropriate function, there is ample room for everything, the light is all that can be wished for and the ventilation is excellent, the peculiarity of design securing perfect circulation of air, and at the same time, maintaining a comfortable degree of heat, no matter what the frigidity of exterior temperature might be. In the matter of convenience, it cannot be excelled, all supplies of hay, grain, water, etc. coming from above, and being automatically conveyed to the stables without intermediate aid.

"The stalls around the building are each lighted by a large window at the outside, and an outer door gives each horse exit into his own separate paddock. This is another special feature and a good one. It is accomplished by enclosing a large area of land around the building from which fences radiate, fan-shaped to the outer fence, giving each horse an individual paddock of about two and a half acres in which to exercise without interference with his neighbors."

There was also constructed a regulation half-mile track in close proximity to the barn. It was kept in first-class condition and provided the trainer opportunity to constantly monitor the progress of his charges.

In addition to the great barn, there were five others of lesser dimensions and more moderate pretensions. Together these provided stable accommodations for about two hundred horses.

The Doncaster Ranch possessed an enviable location within easy reach of all principal towns and cities of the region. Located just below the confluence of the Ruby, Beaverhead, and Big Hole Rivers which form the headwaters of the Jefferson, it was one and one-half miles from Twin Bridges, eight miles from Sheridan, thirty miles from Virginia City, thirty miles from Butte, forty miles from Anaconda, and within easy traveling distance of Helena, Deer Lodge, Missoula, Bozeman, Great Falls, Miles City, and Billings, all cities once united by the railroad. The nearest rail stations in Noah's time were Melrose, on the Utah and Northern Railroad ten miles to the west, Whitehall, on the Bozeman and Butte Short Line of the Northern Pacific, twenty-six miles to the north, and Dillon, on the Montana extension system of the Union Pacific, about the same distance to the southward. It was believed that a line near the Ranch itself would be completed by 1894.

In later years the Doncaster Ranch passed into obscurity. This may have been due in part to an attempt by the Armstrongs to drill an artesian well for the purpose of irrigating the land. The well was made to a depth of six hundred and sixty-six feet and was lined throughout with an inch of steel tubing. The bottom was in a bedrock of limestone, and a ten-inch vein of excellent water was tapped which flowed to within ninety feet of the surface. Further sinking was contemplated, and reclamation of valuable bench lands was planned. The expense of this endeavor coupled with the ongoing expenses of a horse farm of such magnitude was a great financial burden to the owners. Rumor has it that when the artesian well was plugged with railroad ties by a group of mischievous school boys, the concept was abandoned, and the Armstrongs moved on to other more profitable business ventures in Seattle and Alaska. But the glory earned by Noah's horse, Spokane, secured for him and his Doncaster Ranch a lasting place in Montana history. □

5 Bunch Grass To Blue Grass
By Rumor and By Fact

Interpose, a well-bred young mare, looked longingly beyond the fence gate. This morning a lovely spring breeze brought the smell of fresh clover to tease her nostrils. Interpose whinnied eagerly. She glanced knowingly at the unlatched gate hook, and then with only an invisible moment of hesitation, raced for freedom.

Late that evening, a distraught Noah Armstrong, paced angrily the length of the mare's enclosure. The hand who had done this was already packing his saddle bags, but the damage was done. Worried, Noah gazed into the rosy, orange glow of the setting sun and beheld the awesome purple Rockies in the distance. "If I know horses," he said, "she's gone with one of those roving herds of wild horses by this time. There are plenty of them around."

A friendly worker inquired, "Shall we go after her?"

Noah shook his head. "There is too much to do here with yearlings to be broken and training to be done. We'll find her when we want her."

Seven years later, years that passed as quickly as rain down a water spout, Noah had a need for Interpose. This fine daughter of Intruder must be mated to Hyder Ali, an outstanding visiting stallion belonging to the famous California sportsman, James B. Haggin. The match would provide Noah just the "right mix." He instructed his range riders to, "Find Interpose."

The task was not too difficult given the quality of the men to whom it was entrusted. They knew the ways of the wild horse bands, and they knew that while wild horses might wander far afield, inevitably they returned year after year, spring after spring, to the same grazing ground and water holes, drawn there by an innate homing instinct. Interpose was found within a week, clearly discernible by her Thoroughbred lines and deep white blaze.

Quickly paired with Hyder Ali, she was placed in confinement to await the arrival of her foal. Accustomed now to freedom, she did not meekly surrender to her captors, but patiently waited for an opportune chance to escape. One beautiful Montana morning the moment came. Left to graze on fresh bunch grass in a presumably secure pasture, Interpose raised her head to the wind, gave a triumphant neigh and galloped toward the wooden fence, clearing it with ease. Unafraid and eager to rejoin her wild playmates, Interpose thundered toward the Rockies.

Spring was softly unfolding in the mountains when Interpose found shelter beneath the beckoning boughs of an evergreen tree and upon a bed of pine needles brought forth a chestnut colt. There were no veterinarians here, no safe stable walls or warm blankets. This colt was received into a wild cradle under a canopy of stars within the shadows of Rocky Mountain peaks.

The risks of the wild are numerous, as the colt of Interpose soon discovered. One day, while traveling at his mother's side, the snarl of a mountain lion alarmed the herd. A terrifying stampede followed, and the little colt, not as swift as his elders, felt the raking of the lion's claws across his flank. Gathering his long legs in one desperate chance for life, the colt drew away from the danger and found the protective net of the herd and the welcome shelter of his anxious mother. Interpose gently licked her youngster's wounds, wounds that left life-long scars. Such was the first year of life for Spokane, as he came to be called.

The second year, all was changed. Spokane was strong, well-muscled, supple, and agile. He, like his mother, was filled with a wild mountain spirit. It was a great shock to him when he first felt the snaking loop of a rope fall over his head. Spokane instantly began a fierce resistance.

"He's a full-grown tornado," one of his captors gasped, limping off to nurse his injuries. It eventually took six range-hardened riders to bring the fiery colt to quivering stillness. Once caught, he was taken to the Doncaster Ranch of Noah Armstrong.

"I wonder how he'll take to the discipline of racing," Noah pondered as he viewed the arrival of the beautiful colt.

Spokane soon answered him. With eyes alert, muzzle lifted, and a body filled with youthful exuberance, Spokane let his rebellious spirit fall under the kind and gentle encouragement of his Indian trainer. Racing was what Spokane was bred for, and he sensed that it was his destiny.

The above is a nice story, but it is not completely true. It was originally told by Horace Wade for the *Police Gazette* in March of 1951.

Spokane was born to Interpose on the Montana or Doncaster Ranch, popular names for the property of Noah Armstrong, in 1886. Spokane's pedigree reflected back to the kings of both the English and the American turf. His father, Hyder Ali, a dark brown horse rumored to be half-

Spokane, Montana's 1889 Kentucky Derby Winner and Spirit Horse.
Byron Bayers' collection.

Arabian, was by Leamington out of Lady Duke by Lexington. He was an imported stallion brought to this country by James B. Haggin. Mr. Haggin was famous in Montana for his interests in the Anaconda mining industry, and he was also well-known in racing circles, running one of the largest horse breeding farms of the West, the prestigious Rancho del Paso of Sacramento, California. Ben Ali, a Haggin colt, won the 1886 Kentucky Derby.

Interpose was by the imported Intruder, her dam Lilac by Lightning, out of Dolly Carter, out of the imported Glencoe. Interpose was not bred to Hyder Ali in Montana, but at the Meadows Farm of General Rowett in Carlinsville, Illinois. Already, the owner of one Interpose offspring, Grey Cloud, Noah was familiar with the quality of her brood. When in 1885, he had the opportunity to purchase Interpose for $1,000, Noah did not hesitate. Receiving three for the price of one, he bought Interpose, her unborn foal, and her suckling filly, Madelin. Madelin initially showed great speed, but she was injured in training and was sold for breeding purposes.

Interpose never did run away to race with wild horses in the Rocky

Mountains, and Spokane was never attacked by a mountain lion. Spokane found life in the shelter of the magnificent red barn in Twin Bridges and led a pampered existence from the time of his birth. Noah Armstrong, himself, gave the colt the name Spokane. While conducting business in the city of Spokane Falls, Washington Territory, Noah received a telegram announcing the arrival of Interpose' foal. Pleased with the business climate of the city, the welcome he was afforded, and the successful completion of his trip, Noah named his new acquisition Spokane to honor the city so named.

Spokane is a Native American word meaning "children of the Sun." By thus naming his colt, Noah took a step that brought lasting fame to the beautiful and friendly Spokane area, and reality to Indian prophecy.

In the *Spokane Morning Review* of May 29, 1889, Mr. W.B. Taylor, President of the Board of Trade, was interviewed. Mr. Taylor stated: "Since my return, I have learned that there has been a discussion as to the manner in which the famous race horse, Spokane, received his name, some other place claiming the honor. I can give you the straight of it, for I was present at the christening. About three years ago, and while Mr. Armstrong had the Hidden Treasure under bond — the same property that afterward I bought — he came down from the Coeur d'Alenes with George Hardesty. There was no railroad to the mines then, and it was a very rough trip. I went with them to the post office, where Mr. Armstrong received a letter from the foreman of his Twin Bridges stock ranch. He read the letter aloud, and it stated that one of his favorite mares had given birth to a fine colt. Mr. Armstrong remarked, 'I have had such a rough trip, I will just name that colt Spokane in remembrance of the event.' This, certainly ought to settle all disputes as to where the honor belongs."

Mr. Armstrong himself responded to reporters regarding the same question saying, "I suppose naming race horses is a hobby with me, although I like to get good sounding names, not too hard to remember or pronounce. I have horses named Spokane, Olympia, and Umatilla for Western towns where I am known and interested. In naming Spokane, I had two reasons in view, first to honor Spokane Falls, Washington Territory, and secondly, because of an old Indian tradition of that locality which very much interested me."

Spokane's early trainers were genuine Montana cowboys. These included Henry Wetmore, Billy Dingley, and Joseph Redfern. Redfern was interviewed in 1954 by Frank Quinn of the Butte, *Montana Standard Post* at the Fred St. Onge Ranch near Nine Mile. Redfern remembered, "Spokane was a beautiful colt, spirited as all get out. Armstrong hired a fellow named George Foster to break the horse to saddle, but Foster couldn't cut it. I was working there and breaking horses at the time, and I was given the job. I didn't have too much trouble, broke him without spur, and with pancake (racing-type) saddle. Knew the minute I got aboard that animal I was sitting atop a future Derby winner. He didn't disappoint me. But there was one thing about Spokane, he was a little lazy. He'd run like all get out when he had to, but sometimes he had to be forced."

The art of training a race horse in the late 1800's was detailed in the *Daily Independent* of Helena, Montana. The colts were cared for "like petted children." The sucklings were allowed to pass one happy year developing strength and symmetry. Spokane spent this first year in Montana.

In the warm days of May and June, the youngsters with their shabby coats rubbed into smoothness and their disproportionate length of limbs outgrown, were led into an enclosure for evaluation as to their future in the world of racing. Yearlings possessing potential, those with broad chests, short backs, stout quarters, fine blood lines, and sound legs, were selected for more intensive training.

In July, the colts were broken and throughout the summer given gentle exercise, at first, a little canter of a hundred yards or so. As strength and confidence increased, distances were lengthened until when autumn came the horses were ready for their first trial which was usually given in October with two-year-old weight up at distances ranging from a quarter of a mile to three furlongs, but never exceeding half a mile. Just as a young child needed to be watched closely, so did the young horse. The trainer was ever watchful, aware that treatment given the colt at this time left permanent impressions both physically and mentally. Poor handling made a rogue of almost any colt and carelessness resulted in lasting injury.

After October, there was a season of rest. In January, work began again. Like a delicate machine that could be stopped by the breaking of a single cog, the Thoroughbred had to be carefully tuned for his career. Surplus flesh had to be worked away. Day by day relaxed muscles had to be hardened and increased in size. Horses not sleeping or eating were being walked, galloped, or rubbed.

Horses differ in nature just as people do. Trainers must analyze each individual personality and prescribe treatment accordingly. Some horses are big eaters; some are light. One is calm; another is nervous. One must be worked heavily and often; another will be ready with only a few weeks of light exercise.

It was probably in the spring of 1887 that Spokane was entrained by Edwin Edghill to go East to be formally trained near Memphis, Tennessee. Mr. Edghill walked Spokane to Dillon for that train ride. Noah Armstrong wasn't taking any chances.

The year 1888 saw Spokane's entry into the real world of racing.

Trainers rose before dawn and roused the stable attendants who in turn woke the racers. Rubbed hastily and perhaps given a handful of oats, the horses were walked over to the track. The trainer, watch in hand, issued sharp and specific orders to each rider. "Take that brown colt around slow to the five-eighths pole and then breeze him to the three-quarters pretty strong," he might tell one, to another, "You keep that horse going easy until you hit the half, and then send him a mile in about fifty."

One trial was started at one place and one at another, so outsiders had to have quick eyes to watch the many horses on the track and catch any one just at the point where he broke from a trot or canter into an arcing show of speed. When the trainer decided that the horse had been exercised enough, he waved the boy in. Then the "drying out" process began. From head to heel, the racer was rubbed briskly with towels until he was in a glow, kicking playfully all the while. A dripping sponge was forced into his mouth; the cool moisture received gratefully onto the tongue and throat. Next, the horse's legs were washed down carefully, rubbed, and swathed in tightly wrapped flannel bandages. The colt was then blanketed and taken over to the stable. There he was rubbed again in a way only an experienced hand could do. Firm, strong, and brisk motions made the skin to shine like the glossiest of silk, yet never caused the horse to wince from a rough touch. This was followed by a hearty meal and a few hours of rest in a roomy box stall while the track workers ate their breakfasts. Later, tack was polished, cleaned, and mended.

Once the chores were completed, stable hands often engaged in games of chance, went fishing in nearby ponds, or lounged lazily while swapping stories, or napping under a shady hedge. Business began again about three or four o'clock. The horses were taken out for a quiet walk of an hour or more in the grassy infield or any smooth piece of turf within the area. When the racers returned, they were fed and put up for the night. The stable was the home for everyone connected with it. They slept there and ate there. The trainer was constantly available. His orders were absolute.

The expenses of maintaining a racing stable were enormous. The feed for the horses was the best available. The oats were of the finest quality and before being fed to the horses, were sifted and cleaned of every bit of dust. The racing plates (shoes) cost, at that time, four dollars a set, and a horse needed no fewer than four or five sets in a season, and frequently as many as eight or ten. The clothing of different weights for a horse cost from $20 to $30, and each had his own outfit. Bridles cost eight to nine dollars, martingales about three dollars, saddles from $25 to $50, and racing colors from ten to $75. A jockey was entitled to ten dollars for every losing mount and $25 for every winning mount, in addition to his regular salary, if he was engaged by the year. For every two horses, a man and a boy had to be kept. It cost an average of four dollars a week to feed each person. Then there were heavy traveling expenses, entrance fees, and sundries that piled up mountain high, and when all this was added up and subtracted from the winnings, it made a big hole in them.

Multiply these figures to keep them in line with present inflation rates, and it is easy to explain horse racing as "The Sport of Kings." In 1888, Noah Armstrong was the sovereign ruler of the mighty horse, Spokane. □

6 Two For Five

Spokane emerged from his Memphis training camp fit and strong. Entered in a small field, one of only five horses, Spokane made his debut on the Eastern tracks. The carefully selected site was Washington Park in Chicago, and the date was July 5, 1888. A sweepstakes for two-year-olds, the race was called the Hyde Park Stakes. The entry fee was $100, and the winner received $5,560.

The horses moved to the post. Caliente, with jockey Barnes up, carried 105 pounds. Unlucky was ridden by Stoval and carried 106 1/2 pounds. Mamie Fonso, 107 pounds up, was ridden by Winchell. Spokane, carrying 107 pounds, was ridden by Hamilton. A horse named Liberty carried 113 pounds and was ridden by Taral.

The odds were even on Liberty, 2 to 1 on Mamie Fonso, 6 to 1 on Caliente, 8 to 1 on Unlucky, and 9 to 2 on Spokane.

Mamie Fonso took the lead, followed by Liberty and Unlucky. At the half, Unlucky quickly moved into second place, and Caliente advanced to third. As the finish line neared, the three, Mamie Fonso, Unlucky, and Caliente, were even. Pike Barnes, on Caliente, applied the whip. The big horse responded gamely and drew away to win by two lengths. Unlucky was second; Mamie Fonso was third; Spokane was fourth; and Liberty, the favorite, trailed in a tired fifth.

Noah Armstrong was disappointed, but he knew that in horse racing, losing was an inevitable part of the game. On the positive side, Spokane had gained some valuable experience. Armstrong now knew that, to be a winner, Spokane would have to run the three-quarter mile in at least one minute, eighteen and three-quarter seconds.

After three months of intensive training, Noah Armstrong next tried Spokane at the Louisville Fall Meeting. It was Tuesday, September 25, 1888, and the day dawned sunny, cool, and crisp. The track was deemed good, and the distance to be covered was five-eighths of a mile. The purse was a mere $300, $50 of which was to be given to second place. Fifteen two-year-olds were entered.

Princess Bowling was favored to win at 2 to 1; 5 to 2 odds on Laura Stone; 4 to 1 on Julien; 6 to 1 on Englewood and Spokane (coupled): with from 10 to 25 to 1 on the others.

The horses, their weights, their jockeys, and their place of finish were as follows:

Princess Bowling, 112 pounds, Henderson, first;
Laura Stone, 107 pounds, Warwick, second;
Julien, 100 pounds, Barnes, third;
Come-to-Taw, 107 pounds, Finnegan, fourth;
Santa Cruz, 100 pounds, Breckenridge, fifth;
Englewood, 100 pounds, H. Penny, sixth;
Castaway II, 110 pounds, Rogers, seventh;
Irish Dan, 100 pounds, Armstrong, eighth;
Spokane, 100 pounds, Overton, ninth;
Kidnap, 107 pounds, H. Jones, tenth;
Leola, 97 pounds, Ray, eleventh;
Charlotte J., 97 pounds, Steppe, twelfth;
Mildred, 97 pounds, Porter, thirteenth;
Peach Blow, 97 pounds, Britton, fourteenth; and
Select Knight, 105 pounds, Richardson, fifteenth.

Princess Bowling won by two lengths going away with a time of 1:01. It was another might-have-been day for Noah and Spokane. The 1888 season was nearing its end; Spokane had to prove himself soon.

The field for the October 2, 1888, Maiden Stakes included fourteen well-bred Thoroughbreds. The weather was fine, but the track was lumpy. This meet at the Latonia Race Course in Kentucky was an extremely important one. Noah had paid $25 to enter Spokane, and the winner's purse was valued at $1,235. As the two-year-olds approached the post, the odds were: Spokane at 7 to 5, Beth Broeck at 5 to 2, Long Side at 6 to 1, and the others at 10 and 25 to 1.

The horses, their weights, and their riders were as follows:

Long Side, 110 pounds, Stoval;
Lannes, 110 pounds, Barnes;
Louis d'Or, 100 pounds, Warwick;
Sportsman, 105 pounds, Armstrong;
Adrienne, 97 pounds, Barton;
Beth Broeck, 97 pounds, Overton;
Spokane, 100 pounds, Eilke;
Zulu, 97 pounds, Gerhardy;

Re-Echo, 99 pounds, Hathaway;
Franchise, 97 pounds, Soden;
Outbound, 104 1/2 pounds, Moore;
Electricity, 97 pounds, Ray; and
Leola, 97 pounds, Fox.

This race proved an exhilarating romp for Spokane.

Coming from behind, Spokane passed Adrienne, third, and Sportsman, second, to win by three lengths with a time of 1:18 3/4 for the three-quarter mile, a goal set for Spokane after the Hyde Park Stakes in Chicago. The other racers, in their order of finish, were: Sir Edward, Long Side, Beth Broeck, Zulu, Re-Echo, Lannes, Louis d'Or, Electricity, Leola, Outbound, and Franchise.

Spokane raced again at Latonia on October 11. This time the weather was showery, and the track was rated as heavy. Spokane had no experience on such unstable ground. The distance was the ever-popular one for two-year-olds and one over which Spokane had recently proven himself, three-quarters of a mile. Because of his victory, the handicapper assigned Spokane the heaviest weight, 118 pounds, and the odd makers placed Spokane at 7 to 5.

The purse was $400, of which $100 was taken out for second place. No fillies were allowed entry, so the field consisted of nine, two-year-old colts and geldings.

Hindoocraft entered the race with odds of 9 to 5, Tenny at 4 to 1, Julien at 8 to 1, Metal and Red Light at 10 to 1 each, with 12 and 15 to 1 assigned the rest.

Tenny, carrying 108 pounds and ridden by Hollis, won the race by four lengths in 1:17 1/4. Sir Edward, carrying 105 pounds and ridden by Stoval, was second. Castaway II, carrying 108 pounds and ridden by Fox, was third. Hindoocraft, carrying 108 pounds and ridden by Moore, was fourth. Julien was fifth, carried 108 pounds, and was ridden by Barnes. Spokane was sixth and was ridden by Eilke for the second time. Metal carried only 97 pounds and was ridden by Brice. Metal placed seventh. Spectator was eighth, carried 105 pounds, and was ridden by DeLong. Red Light, at 108 pounds and ridden by Overton, had the honor of being last.

It was another defeat for the Doncaster Ranch, but once again a valuable lesson had been learned. Spokane now understood the unstable motion of the wet ground as it gave way under the strain of his flying hooves.

On Tuesday, October 23, in Nashville, Tennessee, on another heavy track and in bad weather, Spokane overcame his fear of the mud and came in first place, a length in front, over a field of seven in a distance of five-eighths of a mile. His time was 1:06 1/4, he carried 115 pounds;

and once again, he was ridden by Eilke. Second place was Long Dance, also carrying 115 pounds, and ridden by Barnes. Third place was Julien at 108 pounds, ridden by Overton. Fourth was Vineland at 109 pounds, ridden by Ward. Fifth was John Clarkson, 103 pounds, ridden by Fox. Sixth was Lone Star, a lightweight, at 97 pounds, ridden by Reister. Last, was another lightweight, named Hollywood, and ridden by West.

Kicking playfully, prancing with grace and handsomely glowing, Spokane reveled in this, his second taste of victory. On this joyful note, Spokane was retired to his winter training camp in Memphis. With intense training scheduled to begin again in the spring, Spokane and his owner now just basked in the warmth of a successful season.

Noah went home to Montana to supervise the management of the rest of his stable, for Spokane was only one of many other fine horses. Armstrong felt good about Spokane's prospects for a successful 1889 season.

Back in Montana, a different stage was being set. Statehood was soon to be a reality, and the newspapers eagerly touted Montana's merits.

J. S. Stevens, who trained trotting horses in Montana for a year or two, bragged, "Everything considered, it is one of the best countries anywhere for breeding and handling horses."

When asked about Montana's cold winters and severe blizzards, Mr. Stevens stated: "Well, the blizzard is a disadvantage, but the general climate, the salubrious air, and the richness of the natural grasses and hay all more than counter balance the evils you suggest. There is another drawback — a scarcity of pure water in some localities, and sometimes the summers are terribly dry, entailing great suffering upon livestock. On the other hand, nature has so formed the land that it affords natural protection to stock in severe weather, and of course, the water question can be settled by artificial means. Everything in Montana tends to give strength and vitality to horses, and I know from experience that horses bred there can endure more than horses bred in other climes. But it is not only the native-bred animals that exhibit this wonderful power, horses taken from the South and West and handled there appear to revive and grow vigorous in Montana air."

In addition to horses, Montana had precious stones and minerals, a benefit that earned her the title of "The Treasure State." These included: gold, silver, galena, copper, coal, iron, sapphires, rubies, oriental emeralds, garnets, agates, amethysts, obsidian, opalized wood, crystals, marble, jasper, slates, argilite, corundum, and even, diamonds.

Fifty acres of the French Bar area on the Missouri River, about 14 miles from Helena, was sold in 1890 to Howard Oviatt and Frank William Jones for an English syndicate. The price paid was $150,000. The purpose of the purchase was the mining of diamonds. A diamond, owned by F. D. Spratt and found in these fields, was cut by Tiffany and

Company of New York. It was valued at $525, and rated by that firm to be of unusual quality. In fact, one expert of the period, Mr. E. B. Northrup, stated, "Montana produces gems, not only of value, but of rare and exceptional worth, quality, and beauty."

Montana, covering an area of 145,000 square miles, or 82,800,000 acres, had 30,000,000 acres cultivated in 1888 and boasted a population of 100,000. Her assessed value was some $70,000,000 — about $437 for every man, woman, and child in the Territory.

Montana produced $35,000,000 to $40,000,000 in gold, silver, lead, and copper in 1888, and her mines paid over $3,000,000 in dividends for the same period.

Montana's wool clip reached 10,000,000 pounds which sold for about $1,700,000.

Montana produced, exported, and consumed beef, mutton, livestock, hides, pelts, lumber, coal, and farm products to the value of $20,000,000.

The number of blooded horses was 100,000, cattle 1,500,000, and sheep 3,500,000.

There were 500 business firms worth over $100,000 each. Of these, 100 were doing over $250,000 and 10 firms were doing over $1,000,000 worth of business annually.

Montana of 1888 had the greatest mining camp on Earth, and the richest capital city in the world.

Perhaps the following poem by Marqueen best bespeaks the proud nature of the period:

MONTANA
By Marqueen

Montana, Montana, the chime of thy name
Rings sweet as a silvery bell,
To its music, its measure, the swift wings of fame,
High-rolling, far reaching, thy glories proclaim
From the heart of each mountain and dell.

Thy high-leaping mountains, so barren and old,
So snow-capped and dreary, the haunt of the wind,
In their secret recesses what treasures they hold,
What marvels of metal, what myriads of gold,
Like visions of Orient riches untold,
Or the fabulous riches of Ind.

Or e'en in each wide-stretching valley and plain,
On thy green sloping hills midst the pines rearing high,
What flocks are there grazing, as though once again
The valley of Jordan, with Abraham's train,
Had found new existence - its once regal reign
Has returned, for the herd cannot die.

Montana, Hosanna! Thy climate serene
On the cheeks of thy people paints roses of health;
With thy soft winds of summer o'er fields growing green,
Where the harvester's scythe, like the falcon keen,
With its flash in the rays of the sun ever seen
Is thy uttermost bounty of wealth.

Helena Journal
Northwest Magazine of July, 1889, Page 7

This, then, was the land of 100,000 blooded horses. Days broke brightly. Chestnut muscles rippled in the sunlight. Copper hues reflected a state's wealth. Spokane belonged to Montana in 1889, another gem for her Treasure Chest □.

7 Derby Dreams

Spokane was ready. He had wintered well, and the fine spring weather made him eager to race. The Peabody Hotel Handicap was held in Memphis, Tennessee, on April 24, 1889. Open to Thoroughbreds of all ages, this particular race was a challenging beginning for the new season. There was a five dollar nominating fee, as well as an additional $45 charged to starters. The winner's take was $1,100. Second received $250, and third $100.

A length of one and one-eighth mile, this was Spokane's first attempt at a route race. It was chosen with a purpose, to give trainer, John Rodegap, and owner, Mr. Armstrong, a chance to test Spokane's ability to perform amongst many older and more experienced racers. The youngest entry, at age three, Spokane had never before faced any of these opponents. The odds on favorites to win of the seven horse field were Strideaway at 5 to 2 and Clay Stockton at 3 to 1. Hypocrite was a 4 to 1 shot, and Endurer was 8 to 1. Despite his two victories in 1888, Spokane was rated at only 10 to 1, assigned the relatively light weight of 100 pounds, and had a new jockey, Monahan. The other contenders went off at anywhere from 15 and 20 to 1.

Strideaway, a strong and popular contestant, was a five-year-old and carried 115 pounds. He was ridden by Pike Barnes, a well-thought-of jockey, used to being mounted on the best horses. Other entries were: Clay Stockton, a four-year-old, carrying 110 pounds and ridden by Taral; Comedy, another four-year-old, carrying 90 pounds and ridden by Abbas; Long Chance, a four-year-old, ridden by DeLong, and carrying 112 pounds; Hypocrite, the last of the four-year-olds, ridden by Overton and carrying 113 pounds; and Endurer, the old man of the group at six, carrying 109 pounds and ridden by Richcreek.

After the flag was dropped, three horses surged to the front — Endurer,

Comedy, and Strideaway. They continued in this fashion through the quarter pole. Then Long Chance made his move. DeLong brought him into second position and held him there through the half and three-quarter poles. Hoping to have enough horse left for the stretch run, DeLong applied the whip but found he had "used up" his mount. The pack now closed in. Strideaway easily cantered to the front and cleared to the finish line a comfortable two lengths in front. Surprisingly enough, he was followed by the youngster of the crew, Spokane. Later commentary even speculated that Spokane could have won the race had his Montana stable so desired. Hypocrite managed third place, while Endurer came in fourth. Comedy was fifth; Clay Stockton, sixth; and Long Chance, the early leader, last. Strideaway's time for the mile and one-eighth distance was 1:57 1/2.

Mr. Armstrong and John Rodegap were extremely pleased. Not only had Spokane proven himself capable of the long race, he had also met the challenge of experience and shown that his youth was an advantage, not a disadvantage.

Every horseman dreams of a Kentucky Derby victory, and Noah Armstrong was no exception. He knew what first place in such a prestigious event could do for his Doncaster Ranch and the value of his breeding stock. A win would prove that Montana was capable of accepting the Kentucky gauntlet, and that bunch grass rivaled blue grass.

On May 23, 1883, Armstrong had come close to winning the Derby. At this, the Ninth Kentucky Derby, Lord Raglan, another chestnut colt of Noah's, proudly displayed the vibrant blue and orange-gold colors. The day was bright and filled with abundant, genial sunshine, especially welcome after the heavy rainfall of the previous three days. Though the track was heavy in spots, and the weather was still unseasonably cold, fully ten thousand people filled the grandstand, lawn, and field. Lord Raglan was considered an outsider and given slight hope to win. He was ridden by B. Quantrell. Also entered were: Leonatus, Drake Carter, Ascender, Standiford Kellar, Pike's Pride, and Chatter. Had this son of Ten Broeck, Lord Raglan, not swerved at the sixteenth pole, he might well have been equal to the test. As it was, he held a strong third, only a half length behind the second horse, Drake Carter.

The year 1883 was memorable, not only for Armstrong, but also because it was the first year Churchill Downs was so christened. Previously, it was entitled simply the Louisville Jockey Club, a name that continued to endure for several additional years.

It had been six years since that first brush with fame; Noah Armstrong knew Spokane had a chance. With anxious hope, he instructed Mr. Rodegap to prepare for the Kentucky Derby slated for May 9, 1889.

Shortly after his arrival in Louisville, Noah noticed an advertisement in the May 5, 1889, *Louisville Courier-Journal:* "Free Derby Day, Thursday,

Lord Raglan, third place in the Kentucky Derby of 1883. Owned by Noah Armstrong. Oil painting by Henry Stull. Armstrong family collection.

May 9, 1889. Spring Meeting. Louisville Jockey Club. Nine Days. Five Hundred Horses. Fifteen Starters in Derby: Proctor Knott, Come-to-Taw, Hindoocraft, Once Again, Bootmaker, Robin Hood, Sportsman, Spokane, Outbound, Heron, Caliente. Among the number: Kentucky, Tennessee, and California for the great stake. Reduced rates on railroads for all points sold first two days, good for entire meeting."

The same paper, in an article entitled, "At Churchill Downs," boasted of the track's condition and touted the fact that more racers were arriving than President Clark could comfortably accommodate. The Downs was freshly whitewashed, and the attractive shrubbery gave the grounds an overall fresh spring appearance.

The white-faced, chestnut son of Luke Blackburn, Proctor Knott, was conceded by most to already own the prize. The accomplishment that earned him such confidence was the winning of the inaugural Futurity in 1888. Nominated in 1885, while yet an unborn foal, Proctor Knott was among only 14 of the 752 original nominees to actually reach the post. For this win alone, he received $40,000 and, by May of 1889, had total earnings in excess of $70,000.

Knott's only major competition was considered to be Cassius and Once Again. Cassius had proven himself a stayer in Lexington by prevailing over a mile and a sixteenth, while carrying 105 pounds in a time of 1:48. Once Again, also at Lexington, was the victor in the Phoenix Hotel Stakes, a distance of a mile and a quarter,

The First Futurity *by L. Maurer, from the collection of the National Museum of Racing and Hall of Fame, Saratoga Springs, New York.*

completed in 2:08 3/4. He carried 118 pounds.

Though cautiously proclaimed, Hindoocraft was not ignored, being considered speedy. Witnesses were impressed by a recent afternoon exercise.

Others mentioned in the press as possible starters were: Castaway II, Badge, Sorrento, Montrose, Libretto, Hypocrite, and Los Angeles. Of these, Badge, at one time considered to be a sure Derby contender, was reported encountering difficulties in training and appeared less of a horse at three than he had at age two.

Mr. McCarthy's California entry, Sorrento, a close second to The Czar in the California Derby with a time of 2:36, was given a more optimistic look. It was said that Sorrento, had he made his move sooner, could have emerged the victor in that contest.

Spokane's Derby trial reportedly was run in style. The Doncaster Stable entry posted a time of 2:42 1/2. That, though not considered a winning time, was indicative of Spokane's stamina, having been accomplished with ease. Noah Armstrong and John Rodegap proceeded with the training of Spokane, ignoring the ceaseless prattling of the press. □

8   A Classic Begins

In 1889, Europe exhibited the first auto, a Benz; George Eastman introduced the Kodak camera; and Churchill Downs initiated the two-dollar bet.

Already termed by sportswriters of the day, "a classic," the Kentucky Derby of 1889 was of such attractive magnitude that conservative estimates placed the crowd at 16,000. Records indicate it was the largest to date, 25,000 strong. They began gathering before noon and continued to do so until after three. From Churchill Downs grounds to Third Street, there was an unbroken procession of vehicles. These were of countless description. In addition to the usual horse or mule-drawn trolleys, the masses boarded for the first time the electric streetcar. This new popular conveyance replaced the trolley by 1901. The street-car lines were extremely long, indicative of the novel attraction they created. The grandstand held 8,000 people, 2,000 more people than there were seats. Another 8,000 gathered in the infield.

Thursday, May 9, 1889, dawned oppressively warm. On such a day, only an important race like the Kentucky Derby could create such an assemblage. Every tongue wagged. The merits of each horse, its pedigree, jockey, owner, and trainer were discussed at length.

It was universally subscribed to that never before had such a crush and jam combined with heat and dust ever occurred at Churchill Downs. Dust accumulated to a depth of two inches between the stand and greensward before the first race of the day had even been run. The black attire of some assumed a cream color, and glossy black boots appeared formed of russet leather.

Corpulent bodies streamed sweat in such quantities that fine handkerchiefs were hard-pressed to stem the run-off. Men puffed like beaten horses, and stiff collars were stuffed into the dark recesses of waiting pockets or fell gratefully discarded upon the grass. Many male patrons sported suits of light flannel and shirts of silk. Straw hats abounded.

Elegant hair styles capped by demure bonnets adorned the females. Many wore white or gray cloth, man-tailored suits. Some notable exceptions to the white or gray norm were evidenced. One, Mrs. Burke Roche, was dressed in a dark blue cloth accompanied by a tiny bonnet, making her appear like the Princess of Wales. Another, Miss Fannie Pryor, wore a pale green cotton topped by a straw sailor hat. Mrs. George Lorillard, the only woman of this time period to own a racing stable, chose black and white gingham for her daughters and herself. Hands were covered by ever-present gloves, and around each waist was a chatelaine from which hung a silver memorandum book, a silver pencil, a vinaigrette, and a little round silver pouch. The pouch was for gold; it was considered by the ladies lucky to bet in gold. The silver pencil was for writing tips in the silver memorandum book. Of course, the ladies listened to the tips, but often they chose a horse for more capricious reasons such as color, number on the programme, some romance imagined upon first sight, or the jockey. Such women often employed a track messenger boy to place their bets. Usually the lad was "decidedly freckled, decidedly crimson, and decidedly tough and slang in manner and speech." The more delicate ladies did not engage in money bets, but rather more polite exchanges of bonbons, bouquets, or other fancies. It was widely held that women lacked judgment in most things except horses which they adored. Ladies gloated over tiny ankles, glossy coats, beautiful curves of figure, and believed that there was no such thing as "too fine breeding."

On this Derby Day getting to the betting shed and booking stands was no simple maneuver. One trip took a full eighteen minutes, and that was achieved only by the implementation of force. Shoving and cursing abounded. No wonder ladies tipped messenger boys; it was not seemly to engage in such exploits. Support for the invincible son of Luke Blackburn, Proctor Knott, created much of this bedlam that continued through the last available minute.

While the more casual throngs of the field waited in the unrelenting heat, games of chance such as thimble-rig were engaged in to pass the time, and itinerant tradesmen busily sought buyers of their fans, lemonade, popcorn, and fruit. Music, too, was presented as a diversion, and for some it was so. Others felt the tunes to be of such "funeral nature" that one man who had made an unlucky bet stated, "I felt pretty bad at losing my money...but that confounded dirge they are playing... makes me feel like I was at my own funeral."

From the turn of the stretch as far as the first furlong post down the track, the paddock was lined with people, twenty-five to fifty feet deep, all struggling to get an advantageous stand near the fence.

Suitable drinking water was rare. Everywhere gentlemen went to great lengths to assuage the thirst of their lady companions, often stopping below the grandstand for beer to relieve their own parched throats. Colonel John B. Castleman paid a black boy one dollar to bring him a bucket of water.

Famous people were everywhere. Some seen were: Colonel Warren S. Reese, Mayor of Montgomery, Alabama; ex-Governor Pinchback of Louisiana; Senator Joe C. S. Blackburn, who went so far as to state that the object of his Louisville visit was the Derby more than the Democratic Convention of the previous day; Attorney General P. Watt Hardin; Secretary of State, Matt Adams; Congressman "Quinine Jim" McKenzie; A. B. Montgomery; A. G. Caruth; W. J. Stone; Tom Stuart of Winchester; Arthur Wallace; and James Givens. Mr. Givens was dressed in such a fashion as to be frequently mistaken for an English lord, discovering American ways and manners. "Diamond Jim" Brady also attended, but the most notorious of all the spectators was Frank James, brother of Jesse James, outlaw.

Spare of build, but sinewy, James was slightly over medium in height and wore a light-colored Prince Albert coat with matching trousers and waist coat. On his head, he wore a soft, white hat of the brigadier pattern. In fact, he was so outfitted that many mistook him for part of the "Blue Grass crowd." Frank James was known to be a "plunger," generally backing his choice to the limits allowed.

Judge Elizah Nuttal of Frankfort, Kentucky, was there as well. He nearly equalled a rather bizarre record set by the former Judge Russell of Bloomfield, Kentucky. Judge Russell had seen fit to adjourn his court to view Dan Rice's elephant swim the Kentucky River; Judge Nuttal adjourned his to attend the Derby.

Amongst the legitimate spectators of the day, there lurked a few vipers in the form of sneak-thieves, pick pockets, and general crooks. Taking almost $2,000, none were caught by the Louisville Police and Detective Department due to the immensity of the crowd. One distraught victim, Bob Miles of Cincinnati, Ohio, lost a cluster diamond stick pin valued at $1,500. He offered a $200 no-questions-asked reward. Another loser, the Honorable John P. Newman of Covington, forfeited his pocket book to the scoundrels. One hundred and ten dollars was lost by Frank Henry of Louisville before he even reached the inside gate. For the second time in four years, Sanford Thurman discovered his "leather" missing. Having vowed never to attend another horse race again following the first time, he broke his oath and came this year. Mr. Thurman now stated, "I hope I will be killed if ever I go to another horse race."

Eleven horses remained of the original ninety-four Derby nominations. The third race on a vigorous programme, this upcoming test of three-year-old excellence, the measure of a Thoroughbred, filled the air with electricity.

The sole determiners of this contest were three. They were: Colonel Meriwether Lewis Clark, President of the Louisville Jockey Club; General James F. Robinson of Lexington; and J.K. Megibben of Lexington. Four timers were appointed. They were: W.S. Barnes, L.P. Tarleton, Major B.G. Thomas, all of Lexington, and Mayor Nolan of Albany. The race secretary was B.G. Bruce. Starter, James B. Ferguson, was assisted by S. O'Brien.

The judges' box sat twelve feet from the inner rail of the track, and it was sufficiently high so as to permit a line of sight on the heads of the horses. A tightly drawn cord stretched between two sighting rods, while the trained eye of the presiding judge, Colonel Clark, watched. Much as a marksman sights a rifle at the head of a squirrel, so the Colonel viewed the finish line. The stand was placed back from the inner rail in order to prevent "missing" a horse finishing on the rail.

Colonel Clark, so aligned, was seated in a large chair. Before him was a small table equipped with all the instruments of administration necessary to complete his appointed task. Before the Kentucky Derby was run, the clerk of scales handed Colonel Clark a list of the jockeys. One of these was randomly selected as the pivot of position allotment. The others were assigned post positions upward and downward from this pivot. Once complete, a listing of the jockeys and their assigned post positions was given to the Assistant Starter, O'Brien.

Colonel Clark also kept a close eye on the betting. He periodically surveyed quotations from the betting ring and compared them to an estimate of chances prepared in advance. If anything suspicious were to catch his glance, a bell was sounded in the betting pavilion and all speculation ceased.

Other signals, too, were the responsibility of Colonel Clark. By one ring of the bell, saddling occurred; with two, the racers promptly moved to the post. After this point was reached, all that remained was for Starter Ferguson to flash his flag, and Colonel Clark to press a button marked "Off."

In the stands and across the field, mysterious nods of intelligence were given "on the dead quiet." Proctor Knott, namesake of a much-admired Kentucky Governor as was his sire before him, owned the allegiance of the multitude. The Futurity winner of 1888, Knott possessed by popular acclaim the title, "Two-Year-Old Horse of the Year." Most of the speculation seemed to center around questions concerning such matters as the distance by which Proctor Knott would win and which racer might claim the second position.

As post time approached, three horses were scratched. These were two of the three Beverwyck Stable's entries, Brown Princess and Castaway II, as well as Sam Bryant's Come-to-Taw. Bryant had entered both Knott and Come-to-Taw, figuring that, if the track were muddy, Come-to-Taw might prove a serious contender. When the day proved dry, and the track fast and dusty, Come-to-Taw was run in the second race of a mile and a sixteenth. In this race, Come-to-Taw was favored, and he did not disappoint his backers. However, the recent run necessitated his elimination from the Derby. Hence, there were only eight starters for the Fifteenth Kentucky Derby. Proctor Knott looked better every moment. Anyone who did not back him was considered "insane." He was to be ridden by Pike Barnes, a scrappy youth, who had guided the enormous chestnut gelding to previous victories.

Strong support was afforded Once Again because his rider was the famed black jockey, Isaac Murphy. Murphy possessed lots of experience, seven previous Kentucky Derbies, including one win in 1884 aboard Buchanan.

The year 1889 was the last year for auction pools until they were revived by Colonel Matt Winn in 1908. They were outlawed then in response to bookmakers' protests, claiming that their business was being handicapped. In auction pools, auctioneers "chalked" the names of the entries on a blackboard. Then persons assembled in the auction ring bid on each horse. The bidding continued on each animal until there were no more takers. Each horse was essentially "sold" to the highest bidder and ran "for him." Horses that could not summon any individual bidding support were grouped as "the field," and bid as such. The total money bid into the pool, less five percent to cover the auctioneer's commission, was paid to the man who "owned" the ultimate winner. The number of pools auctioned off was limited only by the number of pools the players demanded. In the 1889 Derby, Proctor Knott was so heavily favored, according to one account, that the first pool, held on the morning of May 9, brought $100 for Knott and $50 for the other seven grouped as the "field" horses.

Two-dollar mutuel bets were introduced for the first time, and the thirteen bookmakers on hand had a difficult time accommodating the thousands who wished to make a wager. Some assistance was provided them by four "Paris" mutuel machines, a name derived by their inventor in 1865, Parisian Pierre Oller.

Most betters of the mutuel nature were "pickers," timid-two-dollar types, but there were some exceptions worth noting. In addition to the numerous healthy supporters of Proctor Knott, there were eight hundred gentlemen from Lexington who backed Milt Young's entries, Bootmaker and Once Again.

There was a tip afoot that government clerks were backing Spokane. Perhaps this explains in part why after winning $2,400 on Come-to-Taw in the second race, Frank James placed $5,000 on the entry of the "wild and woolly" West, Spokane, after first being informed by a bookmaker

Jockey Thomas Kiley. Rider of Spokane in the Kentucky Derby, the Clark Stakes, and the American Derby of 1889. Kentucky Derby Museum.

that the price of the Montana horse was "Ten-to-one and the sky's the limit." Upon seeing the wad Mr. James presented, this same bookmaker exclaimed, "As far as I'm concerned, that's the sky!"

The closing Derby odds were: 3 to 1 on Proctor Knott, 7 to 2 on Once Again and Bootmaker (coupled), 8 to 1 on Hindoocraft, 10 to 1 on Spokane, 15 to 1 on Cassius, and 25 to 1 on each of the others, Sportsman and Outbound.

Colonel Clark sounded first one, and then two bells. It was post time.

The first horse to appear on the track was Cassius, the only remaining entry of the Beverwyck Stable. Arrayed in dark blue and red silks, sporting a gold sash, and wearing a white cap was the jockey, Taral. Cassius appeared to be a bit "tucked up," the muscles of his flanks tight.

His movements were somewhat stiff, a stature that left little hope in his chances of prevailing.

Next to be sighted were the well-known red and white colors of the Fleetwood Stables sported by Hollis on Outbound. A small ovation was afforded him.

The accounts of the next racer vary. The *Louisville Courier-Journal* states, "...then there came the Montana Stable's Spokane, his legs bandaged, but looking every inch a race horse, as he walked quietly through the gate, and was turned up the stretch, Kiley sitting squarely on the game beauty, with a safe wrap on him."

Thomas Kiley, a jockey of Irish descent, was brought from Nashville, Tennessee, to ride Spokane. Every jockey's dream come true, Kiley had a Derby mount. It was his first, and it would be his last.

Other newspaper accounts described Spokane's greeting as punctuated by derisive laughter and labeled him as small, even "Lilliputian." In truth, Spokane was slightly over sixteen hands in height. All reporters agreed that the chestnut coat glowed like polished copper as it sparkled in the sun's rays, and that in the grandstand cheering began.

This cheering was not for Spokane though. Already the crowd anticipated the impending arrival of the hometown favorite, Proctor Knott, the number six horse to take the course.

After Spokane's entrance, Hindoocraft, looking under-sized, but racy, moved up the stretch. This caused a wave of hope to surge through his few, but loyal backers. Hindoocraft was owned by the Scoggan Brothers, and he was ridden by Armstrong. (No relation of Noah's)

Sportsman, looking the worse for a warming gallop erroneously ordered by his trainer, followed Hindoocraft. The entry of J. K. Megibben & Company, Sportsman was ridden by Lewis attired in orange and green colors.

Suddenly, the cheer that had been but a rumble became a yell that echoed across the upper end of the grandstand and spread to the club house. So sharp were its vibrations that the birds and rabbits for a radius of one mile were frightened. The equine hero of the hour approached. Proctor Knott, the winner of more money and fame than any other two-year-old that ever wore racing shoes in America, was on the track. This mighty horse looked able to run for a man's life. The carriage of his head mirrored his pride within. His long neck fitting into well-placed shoulders, his great depth of girth, the immense length from the shoulder-points to the hip, his powerful quarters and stifles, his long barrel, great cannon bones and elastic pasterns; all foretold the awesome powers that lay beneath the golden coat. Pike Barnes, Knott's jockey, struggled to control this goliath. Barnes was attired in the "game chicken" colors of Scoggan and Bryant. This consisted of a blue jacket with canary sleeves. The jacket bore a depiction of a game chicken. Just barely clear of the gate, Knott lashed out with his white-stockinged hind legs, tugged vigorously at the bit, and unleashed a force that half lifted Barnes from his precarious perch. So doing, Proctor Knott broke from a jog into a long, sweeping gallop as he passed the front of the judges' stand.

Two horses had yet to take the track before the Fifteenth Kentucky Derby began. Bootmaker, the Wilson and Young entry, was the seventh horse to arrive. His jockey, Warwick, wore Peter Wimmer's colors, a blue shirt with white-barred sleeves, and a white cap. Bootmaker's legs were bandage-wrapped, but even without such obvious evidence, it was clear to all that his legs were weak and that he was quite lame. The last horse on the track was Once Again ridden by the veteran, Isaac Murphy. Once Again was owned by Milton Young and carried 118 pounds to the post.

The same weight was carried by all of the entries with one exception, Proctor Knott. One naturally expected that such a Brobdingnag carried more, but this was not the case. The blinker-wearing Knott carried three pounds less than his counterparts. Only 115 pounds were on his back, another good reason why Kentucky was willing to back their favorite son to the point of bankruptcy.

Starter James B. Ferguson slowly cantered up the chute or straightaway and entered onto the main oval track. He left behind a cloud of dust and momentarily disappeared from sight. In only a few breathlessly tense moments, he emerged, his tiny red flag visible in the distance. At the post, Ferguson marshalled the racers into a single line. Proctor Knott plunged and broke like a wild thing despite the severe restraint attempted by Barnes.

Binoculars were simultaneously pressed to the eyes of each nervous onlooker. Blinding dust arose. Everyone wondered what was happening. When the scene was finally clear, it was discovered that Proctor Knott, bolting the line, had reared and danced up the track like a shadow boxer.

Again, the unruly lot began to assemble. Once more, Proctor Knott broke the ranks. This time, he raced better than a furlong before Barnes regained control of him. The feisty, bucking champion proved a hard mount for Barnes. Ferguson's patience wore thin. The audience was restless. Again the horses approached the post. A line was formed. At last, the racers stood.

Beyond the reaches of reality, a mighty Indian chief secretly smiled. □

 Royal Derby

Twenty-five thousand hearts pounded nervously. A drum rolled. A red flag flashed. From the judges' stand, Colonel Clark pushed the "Off" button. Knowledge of the start burst upon the masses. The silent spell was broken. A massive roar split the stifling air; a Royal Derby began.

The first to show was Hindoocraft; Bootmaker lapped on his side. Third was Spokane. The others were packed so closely together that it was impossible to identify them. The pace was terrible. Like a whirlwind, down the straightaway, they came. In the middle of the flying crowd, Proctor Knott was recognized. Near the head of the stretch, Pike Barnes let loose his hold on Knott. Meteor-like, the pride of Kentucky shot ahead making the other racers appear nothing better than "selling platers," fit only for claiming races. Knott held his advantage through the stretch. Without success, Barnes tried to slow the blistering pace, but the golden gelding did not respond. Mouth agape, like a runaway, Proctor Knott ran. As he roared passed the stand at the finish of the first half-mile, his shapely, muscular legs carried him away ever further from the field.

At this point, Sportsman was second, but moving up. Hindoocraft, holding his own, was third. Already in trouble, Bootmaker was fourth. A steady, relaxed fifth was held by Spokane. Running together, behind him, were Once Again and Outbound. Cassius was last.

Through the quarter pole turn, Knott fought for his head, his lead increasing with every mighty stride, five lengths in evidence between Sportsman and himself. Spectators shouted themselves hoarse proclaiming the big colt beyond catching.

The killing speed began to take its measure. Before the turn was complete, Sportsman began to tire, and the noble Hindoocraft fought vigorously for his head while jockey Armstrong continued to hold him a steady third. Advancing to fourth position, Spokane, taking his time, was running smoothly. Outbound was fifth. Behind Bootmaker, Once Again, with the clever Murphy up, waited for an opening. Taral maintained Cassius in last position, but within reach of the others.

The destructive pace grew even more intense, but Proctor Knott had out-raced himself. Gradually, the distance that separated him from the other flyers eroded, and it was evident that they were not coming up, but that Knott was falling back. Barnes, motionless and steady, found only two lengths remained of the lead. Now, Hindoocraft was second, and he moved to challenge Knott. Biding his time, Spokane held onto third. A delicate fourth was seized by Once Again. The others moved closer.

Inevitably, the pace slowed. Proctor Knott was tiring. Relentlessly, his pursuers came on, nearer and nearer. At the mile and a quarter marker, Proctor Knott's lead was almost gone. He was swerving from exhaustion.

Answering Kiley's call, Spokane went after Knott. Like a bulldog, the sporting Hindoocraft hung on, but the mountain-grown lungs of the Montana horse proved too much. Given the go-by, Spokane passed Hindoocraft and closed to within one length of the weary Knott. The run for home began.

Isaac Murchy brought Once Again from behind, and Cassius jockeyed for good position. Outbound and Sportsman followed. Barnes still maintained a slight hold on the Futurity winner's head, but it was too late. Spent, Knott's blaze face veered from the pole to the extreme outside of the track. Desperately, Barnes gathered the tired champion in an attempt to save any remaining speed for the final rally.

Also veering momentarily, Spokane was immediately and expertly righted by Kiley. Holding to the inside, Spokane was followed closely by Hindoocraft and Once Again. Remaining firm, Kiley recognized the time for action. Every leap counted, as gradually Spokane began to reach the favorite. Still anybody's race, the moment of kingship approached. Faces in the crowd blanched as the realization dawned that their native son was not invincible.

Skillfully, Barnes settled Proctor Knott down. The giant chestnut resumed his ground-demolishing stride. Hope returned. But the son of Hyder Ali did not relinquish the battle. Driven by Murphy, Once Again assumed the third position, ready for a daredevil finish. Hindoocraft already under the whip was fourth. The others trailed well out of contention.

The mighty cheers of the early going were replaced by feeble murmurs. Uncertain courage found no voice as the two warring colts fought the "Battle Royal" for the "Blue Ribbon of the Turf."

The eighth pole reached, Spokane headed the fleet-footed Knott, and the Montana Stables' blue and orange colors flashed to the front. Spurred by despair, Proctor Knott's backers found their tongues. They yelled. Barnes quickly reacted. Drawing his whip, he let it fall heavily and often across the favorite's moist sides. Seeing this, Kiley, too, applied the stick. Spokane sprang forward. In seesaw fashion, first one and then the other showing a nose in front, the struggle continued.

Murphy, refusing to give up, urged Once Again to his limit. Inside the sixteenth pole, everyone was applying steel and whips. The wicked rowels plied by Barnes dug bloody furrows into the sides of his mount. Spokane held the lead. Letting out Proctor Knott's last link of speed, Pike Barnes earnestly strove to ward off defeat. Like a thunder bolt, Sam Bryant's goliath answered this last courageous call. Quickly, he reached Spokane's head, but this final valiant rush was not enough. An unforgettable ride by Kiley lifted Spokane under the wire, winner by a scant head.

First, silent shock and then angry wailing came from the watching throng. The decision of Judge Clark was instantly questioned. In what future commentators deemed a photo finish, Clark's judgment was upheld. A daring outsider had stolen Kentucky's hearts and pocketbooks.

The other finishers were: Once Again, two lengths behind the leaders; Hindoocraft, fourth; Cassius, fifth; Sportsman, sixth; and Bootmaker, last.

The greatest, fastest, and best Derby since its inception in 1875 was ended. Running this Kentucky Derby distance of a mile and a half in the incredible time of 2:34 1/2, Spokane established a record that stands to this day. For in 1896, the length of the Derby was changed to the present one and one quarter mile race.

The legend of the Spirit Horse was reality. Montanans raised their voices in exultation.

>
> Spokane! Spokane!
> You are a dandy flyer;
> And you go from Montana
> Where the grass grows higher.
>
> There came from the Rockies
> Far away in the West
> A steed called Spokane
> That of racers is best
> Of all the gay flyers
> That ever was seen
> For he came from Montana
> Where the grass grows green.
>
> Spokane! Spokane!
> You are a dandy flyer;

And you go from Montana
Where the grass grows higher.

    From the *Madisonian* of 1889
       Attributed to Fat Jack

□

10 Making The News

Moments before, lemonade men hawked "Proctor Knott Lemonade." Now, it became "Spokane Lemonade" at ten cents a glass.

A young bridegroom, following the superstition that good luck comes to the newlywed, collected $102 from a four-dollar pool, a wise investment in a copper comet named Spokane.

The racing gentry gathered at the Pendenis Club of Louisville on the night of May 8, 1889. The occasion was the Fifteenth Annual Post-Derby Dinner hosted by Colonel Clark. Elaborate decor, superb food, and impeccable wines attracted elegantly gowned women and polished gentlemen of distinctive class. Recognizing the boiling controversy of his Derby call, Colonel Clark endeavored to settle the matter gracefully. In the center of a giant circle of tables, he had constructed an exquisitely detailed miniature Churchill Downs. Here, tiny wooden horses mounted by equally minute jockeys raced across the finish line, their order determined by the Presiding Derby Judge, Colonel Clark.

Across the United States and her Territories, headlines sang of Spokane's great victory and made excuses for Proctor Knott's unfortunate loss. The *Louisville Courier-Journal* morning headline read: "ROYAL DERBY: Spokane Defeats the Favorite and Lowers the Record. Exciting Finish, with Knott Beaten by a Head."

The ensuing story, punctuated by artist's renderings, described the surprise Derby winner as follows:

"Spokane is a deep chestnut, colt, sixteen hands high, by Hyder Ali, by dam Interpose, and is the property of Noah Armstrong, of Helena, Montana. His appearance yesterday was that of an ideal Thoroughbred race horse, and from his performance it is evident that his beauty is more than skin deep. A small, lean head, with a tapering, finely-pointed muzzle, a light jaw, and large, luminous eyes are the most admirable features of his frontispiece, which is adorned by a white star in the middle of his forehead, and a stripe that extends not quite to his nose. He has a tapering blood-like neck, magnificent shoulders, a deep chest, and absolutely perfect legs, a back of moderate length, a rather light barrel, and stands upon four, small flinty feet, that are, so far as his work has shown, without blemish. His quarters are of the racing pattern, and a pair of clean and well-muscled 'cut hams,' make up the entirety of his personal appearance, save the white stockings that ornament his hind legs clean up to the hock. It is rather difficult to decide to what section of the country the honor of producing the colt belongs, which, in a horsey way, is a perfect gentleman, as he was got in Illinois, foaled in Montana, and trained in Tennessee...'"

Citing from the *St. Paul Pioneer Press*, Virginia City, Montana's *Madisonian*, took exception to the *Courier-Journal's* reported claim that Mr. Armstrong was of Helena.

"We are willing to accredit Helena with all the praise that she has earned by the energetic go aheadtiveness of her citizens; but she need not try to hog the whole world. She might try to leave something for Virginia City and Madison County to which Mr. Armstrong and Spokane both belong."

This argument was an outgrowth of a growing jealousy amongst Montana cities as each vied for the prized State Capital designation. Especially keen was the feud between Virginia City, the Territorial Capital, and Helena, the soon-to-be-named, State Capital.

Another *Madisonian* article continued, stating: "The Fifteenth Kentucky Derby will mark a memorable epoch in the history of American turf. Only in Kentucky and only on Derby day could such a sight have been witnessed. Never on Churchill Downs save once — the great Mollie McCarthy-Ten Broeck race — has there been so vast an assemblage. Never on that now historic spot has there been so great a Derby; never has that classic race been run with greater credit to the winner. It was another case of Himyar Star, another case of Runnymede and Apollo, another case of Gallifer and Macbeth, in which turf history repeated itself." It concluded that, "Spokane's triumph is Montana's triumph. That coming state is doubtless to become the Thessaly of this country for fine horses — a powerful rival, indeed, of Kentucky."

The *Chicago Daily Tribune* banner touted: "Spokane Wins the Derby: The Great Event Decided ONLY by a Short Head." Calling Spokane, "a grand looking colt, just about the same size and build as Proctor Knott," the article then reasoned that had the strong jockey, Isaac Murphy, instead of Pike Barnes, ridden Proctor Knott, the outcome would have been different. Barnes was deemed too much of a lightweight to manage the impetuous favorite. Judge Clark concurred. Barnes himself said, "I ain't big enough for him. If I could have held him, he would have won that race hands down. It was all my fault."

Thomas Kiley, Spokane's jockey, in an interview with the *Nashville American* on May 11, 1889 said of the race: "I was called to Louisville and shown Spokane. The latter's owners told me they did not expect their horse to win, as he had not been going very specially to their liking...They thought they had an outside chance for second money and told me not to press their horse to finish so as to hurt him. I thereupon handed a stable-boy twenty-five dollars of my money and told him to lay it on Proctor Knott.

"When the flag fell for the start I got my mount off well, but was soon left almost in the rear by the others, who were urged on by the terrific pace that was at once set by Proctor Knott. My horse was steadied, however, and laying close to the rail began the long journey to the string. On we sped, Knott still leading and looking all over game and invincible. When the stand was reached it was Knott; at the quarter Knott, and so at the half and the three-quarters. Here, however, Barnes began to save a little and lay in readiness for the final run home. I saw that if ever my time came it was then, and I slightly shook up Spokane and gave him his head. He responded nobly, and one by one I passed the flying animals, Outbound and Cassius, then Sportsman, Bootmaker and Hindoocraft, all of whose jockeys were beginning to ply their whips and bury their steel. My horse moved on and on and soon I had Once Again by the saddle skirts, then I reached his shoulders, then the running became nose and nose for an instant. Another link was let out of Spokane and again he responded. Once Again was passed, and I felt that second money was mine. Just at this time we had reached the three-sixteenths pole, and Proctor Knott who was going like crazy, in making the final round into the stretch shot wide and made a considerable swerve. Barnes saw the danger and piloted like a hero. I had reached Knott under a slight pull when the swerve came. Knott, as he went out, also went forward and did not seem to lose one inch of ground. Up he came and at me, but I was not afraid. I looked back to see where Once Again was, thinking that he was the only one left for me to beat. I have all along believed that if a horse could ever catch Knott in the stretch that he would fail and fall away beaten. But I was fooled. He did not show the least sign of cowardice, but as Barnes wheeled into line, [Knott] came on like a bolt and clung on like a bulldog. It was a terrible finish, but the favorite could not quite catch me, and I won the race.

"It was the greatest race I ever saw and don't think it has ever been equalled in this country at least...I think Proctor Knott a grander horse than ever and have no criticism to make of Barnes' riding. He is a lightweight, and the gelding has a heavy head. I won't say what might have happened had McLaughlin been in the saddle. My horse never lost a foot of ground from start to finish. He hugged the rail all the way.

I consider Spokane a grand horse. There is no danger of overestimating him. He is big and strong and hardy, and I do not think was as fit for yesterday's race as was Knott."

Kiley, speaking with the *Live Stock Record*, also stated: "Though Proctor Knott was the greatest horse I ever saw, Spokane is one of the gamest horses I ever rode, and unless some accident befalls him, he will add other laurels to his name besides the Derby."

Bryant, Proctor Knott's owner, told the *Nashville American* on May 13, 1889: "Barnes did the best he could to win the race, but he wasn't big enough. He is as honest and straight a boy as ever sat on a horse, but he just couldn't ride Knott... A little disappointment is good enough for a man once in a while, and it only makes him try and work harder. If I had won the race with Knott I would have been too lazy to move out of his stable for several days. Now I'll work like a tiger with that horse."

Next, Bryant described how mad he felt after the race. Having worked hard with Knott for the Derby, on the morning of the race he was sitting down in Knott's stall thinking about what a race horse Knott was. "Just then," claimed Bryant, "my wife came in the stable and tried to give the colt an apple, and I made her get out of the stable. When I got home I was blue and feeling badly. I needed consolation and somebody to talk Proctor Knott to. Instead of that, my wife says to me: 'Oh, yes, you drove me out of the stable and then went off and got your horse beaten.' I was mad, and afterwards I felt like crying, but you can bet, gentlemen, that I own the greatest and fastest race horse in this country."

Headlines in the *Spokane Review* read, "Kentucky Broke: a Nag Called Spokane Cleans up... and Smashes the Record." This heroic account continued saying that the only reason Kentucky was not broke that evening was due to the lack of available men from the West to accept her offers.

In Seattle, where Noah was President of the Seattle Transfer Company, parties were held at the Occidental Hotel on Pioneer Place. Honored guests celebrated by gaslight, and the *Seattle Press Times* stated, "It was a joy to the breeders that a horse not from Kentucky could have done so much for racing in the Far West." Considered Seattle's own, Spokane's victory was cause for "cracking open another bottle of sarsaparilla."

The *Fort Benton Press* of Montana left the following quote: "The victory of Spokane - a Montana horse - over the blue bloods of Kentucky is of greater importance to the horse racing industry than appears at first glance. The few thousands gained by his owners was but a drop in the bucket compared to the aggregate wealth the event gave to the products of Montana horse ranges generally. Spokane's victory is a better advertisement for the State than a car load of horse literature. His running is a fact; his beating Proctor Knott - the pride of Kentucky racing circles - is a fact, and his record breaking, considering weight carried, is a fact - all facts, and facts beat theories out of sight."

Noah Armstrong was of as much interest as his horse, being described by the Louisville paper as: "...presumably fifty-five years of age. He is tall and thin, with a pleasant, open face, a ruddy, healthy complexion, and a long gray beard. He dresses well, and in his conversation his sentences are choice and are free from the stable and horse slang picked up readily on the turf."

At the Galt House, Noah conversed with Captain W. H. Williamson and emphatically declared that neither he himself, the trainer, nor anybody else knew how good and true and fast Spokane was.

Captain Armstrong, as this author called him, was referred to as a gentleman of the turf, not just one for whom race horses were a business. His flyers ran for his "gentlemanly amusement and because he has nothing else to do in the summer time." Portrayed as both educated, rich, and honest, "...the acquisition of more men like him would greatly benefit racing in America. He is a race horse owner because he is devoted to the Thoroughbred and the exciting sport of the turf."

Seldom known to bet on a race, $100 was considered a large wager for Noah. Even this modest amount was risked only if the odds were long or the need for creative stimulus arose. Spokane having only worked the mile and a half twice previous to the Derby, was thus not backed by Mr. Armstrong for so much as a dollar.

The pronunciation of Spokane's name was also news. A *Nashville American* source said: "Speaking about Spokane reminds me: We Tennesseeans do not, as a rule, pronounce the horse's name correctly. There is no use in distorting the name of the Montana colt because he beat our Proctor Knott. Now, most Tennesseeans drawl out Spokane's name very much after the style of 'poor whitefolks,' and the gossiper cannot help having antipathy for these unfortunate poor people. You have heard them say S-P-O-K-A-N. He is named after a tribe of Indians in Washington Territory, now almost extinct, after whom was named the Spokane River, at the cascades of which is situated the thriving metropolis of the valley of the Columbia, Spokane Falls."

At the same time, Noah also revealed that he had been offered $25,000 for Spokane. Ex-mayor Nolan of Troy, New York, the owner of the Beverwyck Stable, made the offer. Armstrong was not anxious to sell, stating that he did not need the money and ran his horses for pleasure and sport. When pressed to place a value on Spokane, Noah stated unhesitatingly the scandalous price of $40,000.

In Seattle, Washington Territory, Charles Armstrong received a letter from his father. It bore the dateline, Louisville, Kentucky, May 12, 1889. Published for the first time in its entirety, Noah Armstrong penned: "My Dear Son. Your letter of April 29th was remailed from Memphis and only reached me day before yesterday. I am pleased to know that you are prospering and more than pleased with the place. The thought that you and Frank might become dissatisfied with the place has caused me a great deal of anxiety. Especially as I had been the cause of your going there. Your congratulatory telegram shows that you already know of the great victory of Spokane in the Kentucky Derby on last Thursday. He met and defeated a field of the greatest horses that ever faced a starter, among the lot, Proctor Knott, supposed before the race to be the greatest race horse in this or any other country. The track was at least two seconds slow and the weather unfavorable, but notwithstanding those disadvantages, the race was faster by one and one half seconds than ever was made by a three-year-old horse in any part of the world and two seconds faster than the best time ever made over the Louisville track with the weight up. I am offered $25,000 for him. This is quite a good price for a colt and is quite a temptation. I could make more than that with him this season and have the horse left providing he met with no accident or mishap, but there is the rub. I have until tomorrow at noon to think the matter over. I wish I had time to get advice from you and Frank as I wish to do what is best and find it hard to decide what that is.

"In reference to the mines of which you have wired me, I would willingly undertake to place them providing they have sufficient merit to justify the price asked. Your first message said that you would give all particulars in a letter. This letter has not yet come to hand. I suppose it will be here within a day or two. If you have not already written, you will please send information on the following points: where are the mines situated and how situated as to accessibility, the character of the mines, and the country in which they are situated, the amount and kind of development, the size of veins or deposits and the quality and value of the ore that has been milled, or if no ore has been milled, why not, and any other information you may be able to obtain respecting the property. You know that I never would undertake to sell worthless mines even though they belonged to myself, and I have neither the time nor inclination to attempt it now. Hence, we should inquire closely into any proposition before spending time or money. If I sell Spokane tomorrow, I will be able to start at once. If I do not sell, I would not like to leave until after the American Derby is run which will be some time in June.

"I think it would be a mistake to put Hermine into training as I don't believe her way of going is suitable for a half mile track and then very few horses that have been out of training as long as she, has ever gotten back to their two and three year form. She did not get in foal last year, but she may be in foal now. If this should be the case, of course, you would not want to take her anyway. I will write and explain to Ratton, and he can decide.

"Give my love to Lizzie and all the folks. Yours affectionately, Noah Armstrong. Address: Milldale, Kentucky."

Even the timers were hounded by reporters, error on their part being implied. Some said the official recorded time was too fast, others intimated that it was too slow. One official, Norvin T. Harris accepted no challenge. He emphatically stated that if error existed then "every watch in the timer's stand was wrong." He also discounted the claim by some that "time was lost by the length of time it took to see the flag" as "ridiculous, for sight is too fast to make even a fraction of a second difference."

Hyder Ali, Spokane's sire, found favor in the press as well. It was said that after he retired from the track that he was purchased by Dr. Smith of Louisville on behalf of Mr. Lyon. The price paid being $435, a bargain in light of Spokane's accomplishment.

Everywhere writers expounded on the mountain horse. The *Salt Lake Tribune* pointed out that Thoroughbred breeders must seriously consider Montana's qualities, especially her fine grasses, hay, and grain, in addition to the light atmosphere of the high altitude. This alone, they stated, created large lungs, twice as big as those of horses raised at, or near, sea level. Likened to a forty-horse engine versus a sixty-horse engine, Kentucky or California colts were at a decided disadvantage when contested against the endurance capabilities of their Montana counterparts.

"When men from a valley go up a mountain they are quickly exhausted. When men from the mountains go down to the seashore for several days, they feel as though they had about them a buoyancy which prevented their feet from getting down to the ground. In one case, men cannot get the needed oxygen, in the other, they have such a surplus that it amounts to half-intoxication. We believe that one thousand mountain miners have been arrested in San Francisco for too much hilarity solely because their expanded lungs filled with the dense air of the sea level. They, without comprehending anything except that they felt an indescribable joyousness, were impelled by an irresponsible impulse to paint the town crimson. That was the way Spokane felt at Louisville, and that is why he easily took from Proctor Knott all chance for his friends to make excuses for him, by lowering the record two seconds. It does not prove that he is by nature a better horse than Proctor Knott. The chances are that with the same treatment the Kentucky horse may beat the mountain horse before the season is over, after the lungs of the latter shall have become adjusted to the Kentucky level. But just as a mountain Indian can outrun a valley Indian, a mountain horse when first taken to the valley is a most dangerous competitor for a valley-raised horse. The matter of difference in the lung power of the horse is the chief difference, but at the same time the difference of food must likewise be considered. There is no country where through the long summer the reed keeps more nutritious, the climate is more bracing, or where animals are troubled less by insects; and, while the winters are cold, it is not a cold that reduces vitality. The East and West will have to look out in the future for mountain colts."

On the famous duel, the Louisville correspondent for the *San Francisco Examiner* commentated: "The result was almost sickening to the vast throng of spectators. Most of them would rather have seen Spokane break his neck than the record, and least of all, to win the Derby from Proctor Knott."

Everywhere Kentucky journalists tried to explain Proctor Knott's loss. Most felt it was the fault of his rider, Pike Barnes. The *Live Stock Record* put it this way: "We would not detract from the merits of Spokane, the winner, as he is a great race horse, but we think Proctor Knott the greatest youngster we have seen in years."

While Sam Bryant, Proctor Knott's trainer, searched vainly for answers to why not; John Rodegap, Spokane's trainer was busy explaining why. Mr. Rodegap commented, "Spokane is a colt that has to be urged, but all you have to do is let him know what you want."

The two-dollar mutuels on Spokane paid $34.80 to win, and $6.30 to place. Proctor Knott returned $2.90 to place. No show tickets were sold. The net monetary gain for the Montana winner was $4,880, but the prestige earned was without price.

In the words of Colonel Matt Winn, former President of Churchill Downs and eyewitness to seventy-five consecutive Derbies beginning with number one in 1875, "Spokane was the sort of horse they put in fiction books." □

11 Not A Fluke

While headlines raged, plans for a rematch were underway. Critics called Spokane's victory a "fluke," and still others chided it as "a stroke of luck." Given the conditions of a fair ride and a smooth start, Kentuckians' confidence in Proctor Knott remained unshaken. A chance to resurrect Knott's indomitable image was demanded. Thus only a few short days after Kentucky Derby history occurred, Louisville newspapers advertised, "The Derby Once More: The Great Clark Stake: 1¼ mile: Tuesday, May 14: The Best Race of the Year." A listing of the competitors included: Spokane, Proctor Knott, Once Again, Robin Hood, Hindoocraft, Sportsman, Outbound, and Cassius. As much interest in this meeting, as in the first, was anticipated. It was widely felt that the race would be as good, if not better, as the top three Derby finishers were definite starters.

Already absent from the original field was Bootmaker, broken down from his valiant Derby effort, a distinguished turf career ended at age three. Speculation suggested that Cassius was outclassed, not being considered up to the company of the current stars of the racing world. Senator Hearst's Robin Hood was thought a likely candidate to assume Cassius' position should it be relinquished. Other contenders were expected to come from California, as well as additional Kentucky and Tennessee entrants. At the outset, over 80 nominations were received. Of these, only four would hear the starter's drum.

Named for Colonel Meriwether Lewis Clark of the Louisville Jockey Club, the Clark Stakes honored his role in awakening interest in turf sports, an interest that had severely declined following the Civil War. The jockey clubs of the West owed their existence to Colonel Clark who strove to elevate the standard of racing in the West and to purify the turf through honesty and straight-forwardness. Thanks to the efforts of Colonel Clark, the Louisville Jockey Club bore an enviable reputation even in 1889.

Considered by some to be more indicative of a horse's true running ability, rather than a mere test of endurance, the mile and a quarter distance of the Clark Stakes enabled more colts to ascend the heights of a finish fight. Knowing this, Proctor Knott's supporters were out "for blood," Spokane's blood.

Free public admission to the infield was promised, just as it had been on Kentucky Derby Day. Large attendance was the rule following such a generous offering, and with Proctor Knott's reputation at risk, this rule was upheld. A win was worth $2,510.

Heavy, welcome rains came to Churchill Downs on Saturday night and again on Sunday evening. These torrential blessings routed the dry yellow powder that had lined the race course inches deep. A faster, safer track was expected for the Monday programme; ground elasticity restored, the fleet flyers were thus provided a natural springboard for their ever-reaching hooves. Easy going was envisioned.

On the evening before their climatic encounter, the final starters were named. Only one outsider, Come-to-Taw, found the necessary courage to challenge the three placed horses of the Derby: Spokane, Proctor Knott, and Once Again. With the pace promising to be quick and the competition keen, excitement grew.

The public again backed Proctor Knott by 2 to 1. Spokane, though improved in the odds, still merited only 3 to 1. Once Again closed at 6 to 1. All the horses, except Come-to-Taw, were assigned 118 pounds. Come-to-Taw carried 115 pounds.

To those present, their faith unbroken, it was as though Knott had never been beaten by the Montana colt. Just as at the Derby, they hurried to place their bets; money wagered on Knott was considered as near to a sure thing in horse racing as ever existed. A sample auction pool, taken from the Turf Exchange, showed Proctor Knott at $280, Spokane less than half that at $110, and Once Again at $35. Astonishingly, Knott received even more favor than he had before the Derby.

Mr. Armstrong was pleased with Spokane's jockey, Tom Kiley. Noah believed the boy demonstrated excellent judgment in achieving an energetic and successful Derby conquest. Milton Young could find no fault with the ride of the "Smoked Archer," Isaac Murphy, and considered Once Again's prospects in the best possible hands. Finnegan was chosen to ride Come-to-Taw.

Sam Bryant was not sure of Knott's Derby jockey, Pike Barnes. Desiring a heavier, but still-honest boy, Bryant was reluctant to experiment with a newcomer. The most capable and well-known riders were already engaged, for example, Isaac Murphy. Bryant had little choice left. Deciding more strength was needed and that a change was desired, Bryant hired Ritchie to ride Proctor Knott.

Mr. Bryant's racing strategy remained the same. Proctor Knott was to set a destructive pace that would create an unconquerable distance between the pack and himself. So sure was everyone that this was Bryant's plan and Knott's way of running that, though countless offers were made, no one was so lacking in conviction as to accept them.

Determined by observers to be a stayer and obviously capable of a record-shattering pace, Spokane was accepted as having shown stronger than Knott at the conclusion of the Derby. Spokane's course was true when compared to the exhausted swerving of Proctor Knott.

Close and full of go at the Kentucky Derby, Once Again under Murphy's expert guidance was not going to play a waiting game. This distance was more suitable for him, and the smaller field insured good running room.

Five races filled the May 14th programme. Judges were Colonel M. Lewis Clark, Mr. B.G. Bruce, and Mr. Norvin T. Harris. Timers were ex-mayor M.M. Nolan of Albany, New York, and Mssrs. L.P. Tarleton and W.S. Barnes. Clerk of the Scales was L.R. Ezekiel, and the starters, as on Derby Day, were James B. Ferguson and his assistant, S. O'Brien.

Rain that had begun at 5:00 the evening of Monday, May 13, continued beyond predicted limits, and daybreak on Tuesday revealed a track that was slow and heavy, drying from sloppy to sticky under fair skies. This was fortunate for Bryant's Come-to-Taw, who seemed to enjoy the mud. Attendance, though not equal to that of Derby Day, was estimated to be about 5,000 strong, including a large number of ladies.

As the fractious three-year-olds stood, Starter Ferguson lightly dropped his red flag, and the eager colts were off. Come-to-Taw took the early lead, Proctor Knott second, Spokane third, and Once Again last. At the quarter, Knott's tremendous legs delivered him easily to the fore, three lengths in front of Spokane second, Once Again third, and Come-to-Taw last. At the three-quarters, Proctor Knott still led by a length, but Spokane was a closing second. Once Again clung to the third position, and Come-to-Taw was a hopeless last. Halfway down the stretch, Spokane took control. Determined to leave rumors of inferiority to Knott forever behind him, Spokane, under Kiley's deft, direction, opened two lengths over the pack and crossed the finish line an easy first. No whisker ending this time, Proctor Knott was a definite second. Once Again repeated his show position, and Come-to-Taw finished last, a daring soldier valiantly struggling against insurmountable odds. Spokane's time for the mile and a quarter was 2:12½.

In Lexington, lovers of the turf, who were unable to attend the Louisville races, gathered in large numbers at the pool room. There they heard of the race results from the telegraph. This Tuesday afternoon, the room was jammed for the high-interest Clark Stakes. Received with deafening applause were the two words of the telegraph operator, "Spokane wins."

More than luck, now his critics admitted, lay in the strong spirit and swift legs of the Montana chestnut colt. One thousand one hundred pounds of mountain-bred, bunch-grass-fed energy put the invincibility of Proctor Knott eternally to rest. Excuses founded upon poor handling or adverse track conditions were discounted as Louisville headlines screamed, "They Can't Beat Him: Spokane Gives Proctor Knott Another Beating in the Clark Stakes: The Montana Colt Makes the Famous Chestnut Gelding Give It Up." Continuing in this vein, the reporter claimed, "Proctor Knott is not possessed of the gameness credited him, for he quit like the veriest duffer when Spokane gave him a taste of real horse racing on the stretch." And Seattle banners bragged, "Spokane Repeats: Proctor Knott Far Behind This Time: Kentuckians Satisfied."

Altogether the Louisville meet, according to the *Live Stock Record* of May 25, netted Noah Armstrong and Spokane $9,340 in gross winnings.

Noah said, "I would not wish to sell my colt, and I would hate now for Mr. Nolan or Mr. Van Nest to claim him on my option of $40,000. I calculate it this way... Spokane's winnings should be $30,000 this year. He will have to meet Proctor Knott but once, in the Chicago Derby, and I have an excellent chance to win that race. The great Western Handicap will see Spokane in with 109 pounds, including seven pounds penalties, and nothing in it has got license to beat my colt. Spokane should have no trouble in winning the three-year-old events at Kansas City, and will only have to beat Galen in the Twin City Derby at St. Paul. This horse is well entered in the Eastern fall meetings and another stake or two should fall to him there. He is also engaged in the New Westchester Jockey Club Stakes. The impression seems to be that Hankins (Galen's owner) is after Spokane, but this is not so. Hankins offered me $6,000 for Spokane last spring, but after I refused, he bought Galen for $10,000."

An ambitious program awaited. Spokane was not yet ready to retire his fame so recently won. As the *Spokane Morning Review* boasted, there was "Magic in the Name Spokane." The prayer of Chief Tilcoax, the prophecy of Amotkan, and the redemption of a proud people demanded more. □

12 A King's Blanket

To honor Spokane, the horse, was to honor Spokane, the city. So reasoned the ambitious businessmen of this western municipality. Aware of the unique opportunity created by Spokane's well-known victories, Mr. H. Bolster, energetic entrepreneur and lover of fine horse flesh, devised a plan.

Assisted by Mr. A. A. Newberry, President of the Spokane Fair Association, and other prominent citizens including "Dope" Smith, Ralph Clarke, and Jake Goetz, Mr. Bolster composed a letter to Mr. Noah Armstrong, Spokane's owner. It read: "Dear Sir: Like the growth of this great young city of the Pacific Northwest, the speed of your horse, Spokane, is phenomenal. As Spokane Falls is the most rapidly growing city on the continent, the population of which has increased 20,000 within three years, the young steed who bears its name has shown himself to be the fastest three-year-old on the turf. There is magic in the name, and the speed of the steed is typical of the town in whose honor he is christened. In appreciation of the good taste and sense of propriety displayed by his owner in the selection of this appropriate name, and in recognition of the merits of the horse that has sustained it so well in that distant arena, the many friends of the owner in this city send their greeting and have requested H. V. Bemis, Editor of the *Chicago Horseman*, to purchase for the young racer the finest equipment he can secure in the eastern market, in order that Spokane may be decorated with appropriate ceremony."

This letter was published in the *Spokane Spokesman Review* on May 16, 1889. By Sunday, May 19, Mr. Bolster and his associates had made copies of this letter available for popular signature and distributed subscription lists to raise funds for the purchase of the "finest equipment." These were located at various convenient locations throughout the city, including the offices of Mr. H. Bolster, Mr. A.A. Newberry, and the *Spokane Review*. All interested parties were urged to participate both by personal endorsement and by financial donation.

The *Spokane Morning Review* assisted in this promotion by announcing: "Decorating Spokane: The Fund for Honoring the World Famed Race Horse." The article defined a goal of not less than $500 for the project. Discerning businessmen and citizens were called upon to realize the prominence Spokane's achievements acquired for their community. Eastern newspapers and sportsmen's journals publicizing the famed race horse also advertised the city of Spokane Falls.

As substantial numbers of local citizens desired to make contributions, large sums of money were not sought at this time. The first subscribers and the amounts of their subscriptions were A. A. Newberry, ten dollars; H. Bolster, ten dollars; J. M. Adam, ten dollars; R. R. Moore, ten dollars; B. B. Farthringham, ten dollars; J. Menyard, ten dollars; Clancy William, ten dollars; Steve J. Hay, five dollars; Donald Pearman, five dollars; and George H. Leonard, five dollars.

As notoriety grew for the fleet-footed colt, so too, did the renown of the city whose name he bore. Throughout the land, the word Spokane was heard. Just as the clever businessmen had foreseen, the progressive young city came in for its share of comment by natural consequence whenever and wherever the famed race horse was discussed.

Probate Judge Hartson received a letter from Captain Thomas W. Simmons, U. S. Corps of Engineers, stationed in Washington, D. C. In this paper, Captain Simmons stated, "...Spokane is having a tremendous boon in the East of late due to the grand colt, Spokane. Everybody is talking about him and Spokane, Washington."

In Chicago on business, Jay P. Graves wrote to his partner, Charles F. Clough of Spokane Falls, "People here have lost a great deal of money on Proctor Knott and Spokane. Some are going to change and bet on Spokane in the American Derby here. Most of them will back Proctor Knott. I believe the general feeling is that Proctor Knott will win. Both horses are in the city. The horse Spokane is a great advertisement for our city. If he wins here, it will be greater still. When I am introduced to anyone who takes an interest in horses, they all make about the same exclamation, 'You are from that place that horse comes from that won the Derby aren't you?'"

Acting on a motion made by Mr. Dueber on May 16, the City Council of Spokane Falls passed a resolution instructing Judge Bettis to draft a congratulatory letter to Noah Armstrong. It stated: "Dear Sir: The achievements of your wonderful horse, Spokane, have been heralded to all parts of the world and his name is upon every tongue, but we hope that in the hour of his triumph and of your great felicitation you will not fail to understand that no place has the success of Spokane been hailed with such gratification as it has in the city for which you so

The King's Blanket. Gift of the citizens of Spokane Falls. Spokane's horseshoe is in lower left-hand corner. Courtesy of the Eastern Washington Historical Society Museum, Spokane, Washington.

appropriately named him. We are proud that the banner of our city is to be borne aloft by so noble an animal, and we do not fear that he will prove worthy of his name. It is eminently fitting, we think, that the swiftest horse on the American turf should bear the name of the swiftest growing city on the American continent, a city that has grown from 1000 inhabitants in 1884 to 20,000 in 1889, a city that you knew in its infancy, and of whose future, you had so sure a prophecy that you took the chance of bestowing on it the handsomest compliment in your power. Therefore, as the official representative of Spokane Falls and by the authority of the resolution duly moved and passed by common council, we tender to you and your superb horse the hospitalities of the city. Yours respectfully, Fred Furth, Mayor of Spokane Falls, W. T., May 28, 1889."

As all this correspondence continued, H. V. Bemis, editor of the *Chicago Horseman* and proprietor of the Chicago Richelieu Hotel, searched for a manufacturer in the United States to produce a horse blanket fit for the King of the American Turf, Spokane. Mr. J. H. Trenton was contracted for this purpose. A description of the product was sent to the generous people of Spokane Falls for their approval.

The published account read: "It will be made in the colors claimed by the stable and will consist of a blanket, hood, roller, and roller pad. The suit will be made of the finest quality of blue silk plush and will be lined with pale blue eiderdown and trimmed in the finest quality of orange satin inlaid with Japanese gold. The trimming will consist of scalloped bindings running completely around the blanket and hood. A narrow layer of orange satin inlaid with gold will extend completely around the suit and six ornaments of exquisite design made of the same material as the binding. The lettering, 'Spokane: Presented by the Citizens of Spokane Falls, W. T.' will be worked in raised letters in orange silk thread and Japanese gold. There will also be a scalloped layer one and one half inches wide extending the full length of the suit and on the back. It will be made of the same material as the binding and ornaments. All bindings, ornaments, and layers will be appliqued on the plush with various shades of orange and gold silks and threads of Japanese gold. There will be nothing but the very finest of workmanship used in the making of the suit, and when finished, it will be formally presented by Mr. Bemis on the race track of Chicago just before the famous racer starts in the Great Derby race in which he will compete against a larger number of famous runners than ever before. The appearance of the champion on the track amid the presence of the multitude caparisoned as he will be more gorgeously than was ever a horse before, the approving bout that will go up is better imagined than described, and the name of the most wonderful, progressive city on the continent will be pronounced by thousands of tongues. It will be a proud day for Spokane Falls."

This account taken from the May 29, 1889, *Spokane Morning Review* added that as there had been no personal solicitation whatever for contributions to the fund for the purchase of the outfit, the full amount had not yet been realized. Stressing that this scheme had already netted Spokane Falls the best publicity in its history, more voluntary contributions were urged. Though Mssrs. A. A. Newberry and H. Bolster offered to pay the balance due, it was not considered fair to allow them to do so.

Final cost of Spokane's new clothes was variously estimated between $500 and $5,000. Most later accounts agreed on the $5,000 figure. Certainly, the amount paid was significant, clearly the price of a King's Blanket.

Scheduled to run in the American Derby, June 22, 1889, at Washington Park in Chicago, Illinois, Spokane endeavored to take a brief rest in this interim period of time. Meanwhile, his owner, Noah Armstrong, attended his string of two-year-old racers engaged in Latonia, Kentucky.

Proctor Knott, the twice-defeated chestnut son of Luke Blackburn, was at Latonia as well. Sam Bryant, chasing a much-needed victory, entered Knott in a three-year-old race of one and one-eighth mile. Poor Proctor Knott finished third in a humiliating defeat dealt him by his stablemate, Come-to-Taw. Rumors concerning the health of the 1888 Futurity champion began.

In Spokane Falls, a representative delegation was selected to attend the American Derby. Mr. J. C. Fisher of Spokane Falls left for Chicago on Monday, May 27. He was followed shortly by A. McVey, William Cedar, W. J. Rogers, R. A. Greely, and L. C. Rend. Once there, these gentlemen and other interested citizens agreed to meet on the evening of June 21 at the Grand Pacific Hotel. The agenda for that gathering was the presentation ceremony honoring the victorious Spokane and his owner, Mr. Armstrong.

Hoping that Spokane might again defeat the crack Thoroughbreds of the East, the delegation intended to proceed to the race track, Washington Park, as a body. There, the magnificent keepsake, lovingly prepared, was to be publicly presented. They anticipated that their attendance and the gift that they carried was capable of creating widespread comment in the press.

Montana viewed the enterprising venture of the Spokane Falls' citizenry favorably. The *Butte Intermountain Press* called Spokane the "queen city of the West," and described a circular the citizens had prepared in readiness for their "flooding of the amphitheater of the Chicago race course." The concise document explained the resources and growth of the city and the opportunities available there for investment. Brief, so as to encourage wide readership, it specified the character of the climate, the soil, the agricultural products, the mineral wealth, the extent of the water power, the shipping facilities, the population, the manufacturing already in operation, the extent of the city's commerce, and the improvements such as the school facilities. All this was depicted so that those present and seeking a new location might seriously consider Spokane Falls. One hundred thousand copies were ordered with the cost of such considered minimal in light of the expected benefits to be generated. The *Intermountain Press*, not desiring to hurt the feelings of Butte citizens, hinted at, but refrained from the direct accusation that Montanans lacked the venturesome spirit evidenced in Spokane Falls. The article closed by declaring, "It is a singular fact that the victory of the horse, Spokane, is likely to do the town more good than it will do Montana or any city within its limits."

The night of June 21, in Chicago, at the Richelieu Hotel, not the Grand Pacific Hotel, as previously reported, the Spokane Falls delegation gathered. There, Mr. Armstrong was formally presented the most expensive blanket in American racing history. □

13 Kangaroos, Derbies, And Coonskins

The year 1889 was a dramatic one. Benjamin Harrison was President, and John L. Sullivan beat Jake Kilrain in the last of the bare knuckle fights. It was the year of the Great Johnstown flood and the devastating Seattle fire. Jack the Ripper made news in London, and Nellie Bly began her trip around the world in better than eighty days.

Montana grew from Territory to Statehood along with the neighboring states of North Dakota, South Dakota, and Washington. Of the metal producing states, Montana stood at the head. Her output exceeded $32,000,000 compared to $26,000,000 for Colorado, $12,000,000 for California, and $12,000,000 for Nevada.

Territorial Census reports were hard to acquire, official records often falling far short of the actual number of residents. Far flung and remote residences made counting difficult for government officials who were paid at the ridiculous rate of two cents a name. No such enumerator could profitably hire a team and travel over mountains and plains forty or fifty miles in one direction and possibly one hundred in another to pick up a few dozen names. In fact, such an enterprise resulted in a loss, costing census takers as much as fifty cents a day. Thus, as the population of Montana increased from 39,000 in 1880 to 143,000 by 1889 according to official reports, in actuality the correct figure may well have been closer to 175,000.

On the eve of great development, Montana generated prosperity unequalled. New communities were being born, and money invested never failed to bring generous returns. Mineral wealth, agricultural production, and incoming railroads provided a healthy base to a blooming economy.

In Anaconda, Marcus Daly, copper king, founded the Montana Hotel. The St. Peter's Mission School near Great Falls began. Fifty-three trains went in and out of Helena daily, and Miles City established a superior horse market. Butte got cable cars, and Bozeman vied with others for state capital status. Copper ruled, and Livingston, Missoula, Red Lodge, Neihart, and Sand Coulee, among others, found affluence through coal development. Colonel Broadwater of Helena ordered cast the largest ingot of gold ever made, valued at $100,000 and placed on exhibit at the Minneapolis Exposition. Great Falls generated hydroelectric power through the building of Black Eagle Dam, and the Boston and Montana Consolidated Copper and Silver Mining Company located its smelting and refining works there.

The Northern Pacific Railroad brought visitors regularly to Yellowstone Park, and there they experienced an excellent hotel system, a perfect line of stages, well-built government roads, and natural scenery of phenomenal variety.

John Quickbonner, while bathing in Gold Creek, found a dozen large gold nuggets. A rush began from Grantsdale, Missoula County, and within three hours, every able man in town was off to the new discovery. Brick businesses and street cars were planned for Missoula.

Estimated at 15,000 in number, Montana's Indian population suffered a similar plight to that of other noble tribesmen; the destruction of their hunting grounds, the elimination of the bison, and the loss of their homelands. Sitting Bull, Sioux medicine man and visionary of the Custer Battle of the Little Bighorn, was critically ill with pneumonia on the Standing Rock Reservation of South Dakota, his days of glory but a fading memory, cherished within a brave heart.

When asked whether he believed terms were possible concerning the sale of Sioux lands to the white government, the Sioux Chief Red Cloud answered with pathetic humor: "Oh, yes, I think we shall sell the lands."

"But where will the Sioux go then?" asked the concerned interrogator.

"Well," replied Red Cloud, "the circus season is just coming on, there are about enough Sioux left to go around, and I think we will go into that business."

The opening of the Broadwater Hotel in Helena gave birth to Montana's health resort industry. Touted as being a Mecca of relief for sufferers of pulmonary diseases, Montana gained fame as a land of almost constant sunshine, exceptionally clear air, and cloudless days where unblemished blue heavens capped glorious mountains. Germs, it was said, did not prosper well in her dry, rarefied atmosphere.

Dr. C. K. Cole of Helena, President of the Territorial Legislative Council, cited several healthful advantages inherent in Montana living, ". . . the breathing capacity of persons who have not reached adult life, coming from sea level, is increased one-third after a residence of a few years. There is peculiar influence on certain nervous temperaments and diseases which is not fully understood as yet. . . I am also satisfied that mental activity is, at least temporarily, increased and intensified here in a manner similar to the effect of alcoholic stimulation."

Several enthusiastic sportsmen seriously considered the importation of kangaroos into Yellowstone Park. Extinction of the buffalo having left the plains without big game of any importance, they believed the Australian kangaroo to be a proper replacement. Hunting the kangaroo was promoted as being second in excitement and interest only to killing the buffalo. Supporters anticipated great commercial gain from the sale of products made of kangaroo leather, and as the animals bred rapidly only a few years of government protection was considered necessary before this rare sport might widely be enjoyed. Still other creative souls asked the question, "Are Gophers Good to Eat?"

It was amid this atmosphere of unrestrained opportunity that Spokane ascended to his proper role as King of the American Turf, at last amassing enough confident fans to rate the status of favorite in the betting parlors.

Bigger than the Kentucky Derby or the Belmont Stakes in 1889, the American Derby was the richest three-year-old classic in the country. Its winner received the enormous sum of $15,440. California sportsmen dominated this Chicago Derby consecutively from 1885 to 1888 with the fine horses: Volante, Silver Cloud, C. H. Todd, and the Emperor of Norfolk. The competition in this Derby consisted of the best racers in the country at this time. It was a test of the great to determine the greatest, and everyone wanted a chance to run.

As early as June 3, the preparatory gossip for the event began. A big field was eligible, 147 nominations having been received. Even mediocre horses, encouraged by rules that penalized past winners by weight and provided allowances for maidens, flocked to Chicago. On June 6, a published account recorded the odds of sixty-eight possible contenders.

Many wished that Spokane and Proctor Knott were not entered, or that they were not such heavy favorites. A telegram received in Louisville falsely stated that Spokane had broken down while being worked at Washington Park, and that neither he nor Proctor Knott would start for the American Derby. Supposedly originating from the *Sporting World* of New York, the contents were ascertained to be incorrect as Spokane had not yet arrived at Washington Park.

Touts, employees of bookmakers and often independently solicitous, inhabited the barns and stable roof tops. Their job was to spy on the trials of horses and watch young colts as they took their exercise. The unraveling of stable secrets was their goal, and the information they gathered was disclosed to bookmakers who then influenced the odds and provided tips to paying customers. Some were reliable; others were not.

In the Chicago races, weights carried were determined not by age, but by handicap. A debate over this method surfaced. Gamblers desired that good animals be anchored by weight, thus making betting against the favorites possible. Breeders argued that such a system negated the need for one to breed a better horse since first-class flyers would be dragged down to the level of the inferior by increased weight classification. A remedy was sought that would preserve the continued refinement of the Thoroughbred strain.

Sam Bryant disagreed with the jockey clubs on another point. He sought redress from the Turf Congress on the question of allowing owners to enter stakes by paying their entry fees "in paper" promises. Winners then had the unwelcome task of collecting, and quite often they were forced to absorb forfeits as losers failed to honor claims justly made of them. Few friendships survived the harsh feelings that often surfaced, as even fair remunerations were seldom paid willingly. Bryant urged the cash-entry plan.

Proctor Knott, Sam's golden goliath, somewhat diminished in size by recent losses, prepared for his third meeting with Spokane. Saying that his horse would go to the post fit, or not go at all, Sam felt strongly that all that stood between Knott and success was a proper ride. In contrast, those that thought Proctor Knott lacked speed welcomed another chance to bet against him, and the increasing number of turfites who believed Bryant's horse suffered from a deficiency in drive looked forward to having their suspicions confirmed. Though Knott's position was not at all without hope, it was considered by many to be his last chance for redemption before earning "dunghill" status among the betting populace.

Appearing rather light in flesh, Proctor Knott still held the affection of Kentucky citizens. They journeyed daily to his comfortable and roomy box located just outside the grounds of Churchill Downs. On June 10, at Sam Bryant's private stable, formerly the property of the Applegates and located to the rear of his son-in-law Ott's grocery on Fourth Street, Proctor Knott patiently awaited his transfer to Chicago one week hence along with his stable companions, Come-to-Taw and Benedict. The white-faced chestnut was sufficiently recovered from his illness of the last month to warrant Bryant's continued confidence. Fighting the duffer label and charges that his son of Luke Blackburn owned a chicken-heart, Sam stated that Knott "would show a mile and a half before the snow flies that is fast enough to set aside all doubt as to the gelding's ability to race." Not satisfied with Barnes' Kentucky Derby ride and lukewarm about Finnegan's performance in the Clark Stakes, Sam Bryant continued searching for a better jockey. Unfortunately, Isaac Murphy was still committed to Once Again, though he was credited with so many mounts that the *Louisville Courier-Journal* of June 9 suggested, "If Isaac rides all the horses that report has given him, he will have no trouble in getting a circus engagement when too heavy for the pig skin."

Assigned a three-pound penalty, Spokane carried 121 pounds, Come-to-Taw, also under penalty, but as a gelding, bore 118 pounds. Don Jose and Once Again were rated equal to Spokane. And at 115 pounds, Proctor Knott, having no penalty, gained a six-pound advantage over his Montana rival. Bookmakers made Proctor Knott, Spokane, and Sorrento early favorites. Spokane rightfully topped the odds, but Proctor Knott found favor among private opinion counts.

June 17, 1889, Proctor Knott and Come-to-Taw left Kentucky for Illinois. Sam Bryant carefully and ceaselessly cared for his prized gelding, and though Knott still appeared light in flesh and not up to a grueling mile and one half run, his owner remained trusting of his chances. The boastful Bryant strongly desired to restore Knott's reputation and nullify the rudely persistent comments impugning his character.

A corresponding veterinary surgeon wrote that courage in a horse was related to his color saying, ". . . having performed thousands of operations on horses, some of them sufficiently painful to test the gameness of the subject, I have found that the most arrant cowards among horses are sorrels, and the gamest bays or browns. Some time ago, I performed an operation on a pair of sorrels, and they groaned like human beings. A bay or brown will usually suffer without a noise of any kind, just rolling its big eyes in an appealing way which is almost human in its intensity. Gray and white horses as a rule are not particularly game."

Proctor Knott and Spokane were both chestnuts, possibly even sorrels if such color was recognized by the Thoroughbred registry. Thus, at least in this case, the veterinary's theory failed to reach a verifiable conclusion. It was not Proctor Knott's color that determined his seeming lack of fight, nor was it Spokane's hue that determined his ready stamina.

As the date of the great race neared, many pretenders withdrew, the company a class beyond their abilities. Such casualties included: Galen, French Park, and Louis P., who pulled up lame. Also, the highly acclaimed Salvator, who unfortunately threw a splint, was scratched. Sorrento's backers wished for rain, assertively expressing that in their opinion, "There are not enough horses in the world to beat Sorrento in the mud."

Described as "playful as a kitten," Spokane had been galloped regularly, but not raced. He was in splendid condition and ready for any amount of work. Trotting at the start of his workouts, his action indicated some lameness, but this quickly disappeared after about a few hundred yards as he squared away and sped smoothly onward.

John Rodegap, Spokane's trainer spoke thusly: "He's lame I know. At least, they all say he is lame, but he is no lamer than he was when he won the Kentucky Derby and the Clark Stakes at Louisville. In trotting, he goes clumsily at first, having a sort of flop, and every time that he is seen at it away goes the report that he is lame. The morning before he won the Clark Stakes, he was noticed flopping along, and the trainers and owners began touting him as dead lame and having no chance to win."

Brood Church of the *Spirit of the Times* liked the prospects of Don Jose whom he described as a "...grand looking animal, over sixteen hands high and with a tremendous stride."

On Tuesday, June 18, Proctor Knott and Come-to-Taw arrived in Chicago under the particular care of their determined owner. At the Washington Park track, Knott worked lightly, his last fast run having occurred earlier in Louisville. Watches had held that attempt to be well inside 2:40.

Local experts felt that Proctor Knott did not look as well as he should and was not sufficiently recovered from his recent illness to effectively compete over the required route. They predicted a better finish for Come-to-Taw than Proctor Knott.

Secretary Brewster of Washington Park was in a quandary over the housing of all the potential contenders. Twenty-six days of racing were planned, and $100,000 in prizes made this particular meet one of high interest to stables throughout the United States. Only 708 stalls were available, and preference was assured the stakes horses. Additional stalls were hastily constructed to accommodate the overflow of purse entries.

J. B. Haggin was in Chicago. He expected to enter Fresno into the fray, since his great Salvator had been withdrawn. The wealthy Mr. Haggin owned Kentucky Derby honors with Ben Ali in 1886. At that time, Haggin desired to back his colt with thousands of dollars, but the absence of bookmakers on the track at Louisville prevented him from doing so. He made his objection known to the director and threatened to withdraw his entire stable if matters were not remedied. When the Louisville Jockey Club responded negatively, Mr. Haggin did as he had warned. Being a regular and respected participant in the Eastern racing circuit, Haggin found many supporters there. The Western circuit's Kentucky Derby, which had been well attended from its inception in 1875, suffered tremendously in ensuing years because of the Haggin incident. A very influential Californian, whose great stallion Hyder Ali was the sire of the American Derby favorite Spokane, Mr. Haggin and his entries were always afforded much respect.

By June 20, the *Chicago Daily Tribune* reported that the original list of 147 nominations had been pared down to 70. Of these, only nineteen were listed as probable starters. These were:

    Beverwyck Stable's brown filly, Brown Princess;
    J. J. Carter's chestnut colt, Kasson;
    Fleetwood Stable's chestnut colt, Outbound;
    Walter Gratz's bay colt, Blue Rock;
    John Good's bay colt, Vidette;

J. B. Haggin's bay colt, Fresno;
Labold Bros.' brown filly, Retrieve;
Montana Stable's chestnut colt, Spokane;
Maltese Villa Stock Farm's bay colt, Flood Tide;
D. J. McCarty's chestnut colt, Sorrento;
J. K. Megibben's chestnut colt, Sportsman;
W. Mulkey's brown colt, Le Premier;
G. M. Rye's bay colt, Long Dance;
M. D. Richardson's chestnut colt, Teuton;
J. R. Ross' bay colt, Gladstone;
Scoggan and Bryant's bay colt, Come-to-Taw;
Scoggan and Bryant's chestnut gelding, Proctor Knott;
Theodore Winter's chestnut colt, Don Jose;
and Milton Young's bay colt, Once Again.

Johnny Campbell of the Beverwyck Stables believed Brown Princess capable of the distance, in light of past performances and times.

John Carter, a shrewd man of the turf, received favorable word from his trainer which warranted shipping Kasson from the east to Chicago.

Public opinion of Outbound was low, but his owner, L. P. Tarleton, declared that his horse would start.

Though winner of a three-quarter mile dash at New York's Jerome Park, Blue Rock was not considered dangerous.

Vidette's trainer, Dad Allen, pronounced his charge well and doing fine.

Mr. Haggin's Fresno, though successful as a two-year-old, was believed to lack the form he possessed then. Haggin was hesitant to ship Fresno unless he proved worthy. C. H. Todd, formerly of Haggin's Rancho del Paso, was the 1887 American Derby winner, and many felt that if Haggin did bring Fresno, he could be counted upon to have a chance.

Montrose won the Kentucky Derby in 1887, and Retrieve was his sister. Retrieve reputedly worked the mile and a half faster than any of the other Derby candidates. She deserved a look.

Flood Tide, a doubtful starter from California, was being treated for a splint. Mike Kelley, his trainer, understandably let up on him. However, his owner, Porter Ashe, decided that if anything close to fitness was ascertained before Saturday, the colt, a speed horse and considered by others to be ill-equipped for the weight and distance of the American Derby, was to start.

Dan McCarty, known for his ever-present white hat, placed his reputation on Sorrento, a brother of C. H. Todd (now owned by McCarty). Sorrento was well-muscled and fit, but rather small in stature, only fifteen hands, one and one-half inches in height. His trainer, Buchanan, cared for him well.

Only the uncertainties of horse racing could justify Sportsman's entry.

He was not judged to be of the quality necessary to seriously threaten the high-class foes aligned against him in the Derby.

Le Premier, who only won his first race of the season a week previously, and who appeared "not right" in the beginning, was rumored to have attained his true form and promised to show himself "a great race nag."

Raced only a week ago in St. Louis and considered above average as a race horse, Long Dance was expected to "cut a big swathe in almost any company."

Even his owner, Hardy Durham, thought Teuton out-classed. The only justification offered for his possible start was the desire of Hardy to see his colt run.

Bryant's Proctor Knott was expected to again set a killing pace and to run in front as long as he could. Bets of even money that Proctor Knott would beat Spokane were made. Come-to-Taw, Bryant's other entry, was widely respected as well.

Don Jose beat Sorrento three times at equal weights, and his groom Albert Cooper emphatically declared, "Dat hoss can beat anybody's hoss in de mud. De all rated Sorrento a cracker jack in the mud and that fall when he got back to de coast to his Don Jose in de mud 'twant no race at all. Don Jose ran right away from him at de finish." Though Mr. Winter scratched Don Jose on account of a heavy track in St. Louis, he was quietly assured that his colt was a definite factor in the upcoming Derby.

Troubled by rheumatism in the early spring, Once Again seemed to be extending himself now, and appeared much improved.

Strong feelings about the horses surfaced Thursday morning, June 20, when Dad and William Allen, trainers of California Senator Hearst's string, argued with Brown Dick, Once Again's trainer, over the merits of Proctor Knott. The elder Allen asserted that Proctor Knott was the greatest horse that he ever saw, and that with a fast track he would be the only horse in the American Derby. Trainer Murray defended his colt, declaring that Once Again would best Proctor Knott. Allen then became so indignant that he could not keep from stammering, and walked away. Shortly afterward, Spokane came out followed by his owner and trainer. Murray shared the topic of the argument with John Rodegap. Mr. Rodegap responded, "Well, you bet him fifty for me that Once Again beats Proctor Knott, and if that don't suit him, you can make it a hundred."

Whereupon Noah Armstrong added, "Once Again, hey! That fellow is liable to beat anybody's horse."

Of Spokane, John Rodegap commented, "I don't see how a horse could be doing better. He has that limp which I suppose is something and will develop in time, but it is just as it was when he won the Derby and the Clark Stakes, and doesn't appear to be at all troublesome. What it is nobody seems to know. I don't like it, but am satisfied so long as it doesn't affect him. He'll run a good race, and I will be disappointed if he doesn't win. It has been said that he couldn't run on a hard, fast track. All there is to that is he hasn't been asked to run on a track of that kind. Every time I have asked him to do anything I have always found him able to do it."

A Kentucky turfman, speaking of Saturday's big race, announced his choice, "Down in Kentucky whenever a man wants to be classed as a good hunter he's got to show his coonskins. Whenever anybody begins telling about a great hoss somebody will ask, 'Whar's his coonskins?' That fellow Spokane has done got his coonskins, and I reckon he's a good hoss, good enough to get some more. My money goes on the fellow that can show the skins." □

14 Pre-Race Trials And Predictions

The candidates were in full training for Saturday, June 22, and the running of the great American Derby. On Wednesday morning the two California entries, Sorrento and Don Jose, worked out.

Sorrento made his move early in the day and rated a time of 3:05. He ran on the extreme outside of the course where the footing was tough and rough, but he finished strong and cooled off nicely. He appeared clean and fit. His trainer, Buchanan, desired him heavier by about thirty pounds. Others disagreed. They felt that Sorrento had an abundance of muscle, his every line reflecting substance and power. Buchanan's major concern was the rider, for he did not yet know if one had been engaged.

Don Jose did not take the track until nearly 11 o'clock. The sun and wind had dried the track making it faster than when Sorrento had run. Accompanied by his stable companion, Joe Courtney, Don Jose covered the ground in 2:59 1/2. Eyewitnesses said that he "ran like a race horse."

One trainer remarked, "He's hot goods and no mistake."

Not judged to be as large or as good looking as his full brother, Ed Corrigan, Don Jose was trimly built. His conformation defined speed, but his brother's reputation for not going the 1 1/2 mile followed him. Vowing that Don Jose was a stayer, his owner and trainer were confident in his abilities.

Banneret was galloped only a mile, and he pulled up lame. George Cadwallader, nicknamed "Cad," admitted, "He always does. He had osselets on his ankles, and they make him sore every time he works."

Spokane did not run on Wednesday. Trainer Rodegap stated, "I worked him yesterday because I was afraid we would never have any more fine weather, and I suppose I made a mistake. He appears to be all right, though, and I think he'll give a good account of himself Saturday."

Noah Armstrong declared, "I guess he'll be all right now. We have just got some good oats for him. We had them sent from Montana. Just look at them and feel their weight. I don't see how they can beat him now."

Firm and elastic of step, Spokane defied persistent rumors that he was lame. Because he was not worked, many believed Rodegap was afraid to work Spokane strongly. Despite this, he was still a money favorite in Chicago.

Proctor Knott's eye was bright. His coat shone with a healthy brilliancy, and his superb racing condition was visible to even the least experienced. As he proudly commanded his stall, Proctor Knott appeared ready to snatch Spokane's crown. Sam Bryant wished him somewhat heavier, feeling that if the Derby were a week further off, Knott's chances would be guaranteed:

"He was a sick horse in Louisville, and I couldn't tell what was the matter with him. It was after he ran in the Clark Stakes. He was all right in the morning and deathly sick that night. He's coming around all right now, and will run a good race Saturday. The only thing I'm afraid of is he'll weaken at the finish.

"I'll give you a tip. The fellow that follows him a mile or a mile and a quarter won't win. He may win by setting the pace, but none of those others can win if they try to keep up with him. There's no use talking about not setting the pace. If I won't do it somebody else will and my hoss don't want to let any other hoss cut out the work for him. He is the quietest hoss you ever saw in a stall. On the track, he's just like his daddy — wants to do everything in a minute, and come as near doin' it as anybody's hoss when he's right. He ought to have won the Kentucky Derby. It was the greatest Derby ever run, but that don't count — he ought to have won it. I never felt so sore about anything. Barnes lost the race. He couldn't ride him, but he was the best boy I could get. When he got into the stretch he swung clear to the outside. If he had kept going straight he couldn't have lost. Barnes never could ride him. He's not a hard hoss to ride. All a boy has to do is let him go away at the start and then take a steady pull on him and remain still. Barnes never could keep his head up after he had gone half a mile. He wasn't strong enough. There ain't but three or four riders in America. I offered Murphy $1,000 to ride this hoss in this Derby and couldn't get him. He is going to ride Once Again, and I don't know who I'll get to ride. There's a hoss there, Come-to-Taw. With a good boy on him, he'd have a good chance. He is game as they make 'em. I honestly believe Murphy could win this Derby with him."

Spokane, Proctor Knott, Once Again, Long Dance, Banneret, and Vidette ran their final preparations on Thursday. Using the outside of the track, which was at least three seconds slow, the actual distance traveled by each well excelled the regulation mile and one-half distance of Saturday's upcoming Derby.

Once Again scored the best time, 2:51. He ran in good style and pulled up without any signs of distress. A fine race was expected with Murphy as his pilot.

Spokane worked at 2:53 1/4. He appeared unworried, and he did not pull up lame. Friends, on witnessing this practice, believed Spokane would be the only horse left in the race after the last eighth pole was passed. His trainer was delighted with Spokane's cooling out, for after it he showed as much spirit as if he had only been out for a walk. Mr. Rodegap looked forward to a great Derby performance.

Under gathering clouds, Proctor Knott's work began. By the finish, a light shower was falling. Sam Bryant was not pleased by this, Knott's time being 2:53 1/2, a quarter of a second slower than Spokane's. One observer said, "He'll go fast in the Derby."

Another said, "He's just as fast as he was when Spokane beat him for the Kentucky Derby."

Sam Bryant commented, "The judges said Spokane beat him, but I'll never believe that until I die. The judges' decision had to go, that's what they were there for; but lots of people could see just as well as the judges and they told me my hoss won."

In response, John Rodegap spoke, "Proctor Knott came near winning because he swerved to the outside. The footing on the inside was soft; on the outside, it was hard. If he had remained alongside of my horse and finished with him in heavy going, he would have been beaten by two or three lengths. By swerving, he struck hard ground, on which he could go along much easier, and that's how that game finish, as it is called, came about."

Vidette was reported doing the mile and a half in 2:58. Though his owner was pleased with this performance, he declined to state positively that Vidette would start.

Banneret and Long Dance only moved a mile and a quarter during these pre-race workouts. George Cadwallader said Banneret's run did not suit him, and that as a result, Banneret would not start. Long Dance, though his time was not available, ran easily. Cadwallader picked him as a definite starter.

Bad news was announced on Friday. Benedict, Sam Bryant's four-year-old colt, was involved in a track collision at Washington Park. After taking his morning gallop along the inside track accompanied by four others of the Bryant string, Benedict was being walked the wrong way of the track near the outside rails. George Hakes' colt, Ira E. Bride, was speeding along the outside, where he safely passed four of Bryants' racers, just missing the great Proctor Knott. Unfortunately, Benedict was not missed. He was struck forcefully on the hip, the intensity of the blow causing him to fall to the ground, breaking his back. To end his suffering, Benedict was shot. The fast and magnificent chestnut gelding was valued at $12,000, but his worth to Bryant went without price. Such pre-Derby luck did not bode well for Proctor Knott's owner.

Eleven hopefuls remained in the running, and depending on which paper one read, a crowd of between 20,000 and 40,000 was expected. All of the sixty-eight private boxes available were sold out. Never in the history of racing had as many good Thoroughbreds faced the starter: Spokane, Proctor Knott, Once Again, Don Jose, and Sorrento, not to mention such long shots as: Retrieve, Outbound, Sportsman, Le Premier, Come-to-Taw, and Long Dance.

As the first big American Derby pool closed in Louisville at the Turf Exchange, Proctor Knott sold for $325 and Spokane for $200. Kentuckians refused the Montana horse top billing. Next in line was Don Jose, $100 and carrying 121 pounds. Then was Sorrento, $65, rated at 118 pounds. Once Again with 121 pounds up brought $35, and Retrieve under a three-pound penalty, 116 pounds up, brought $20. Sixteen dollars was given for Long Dance with 118 pounds. Outbound, Le Premier, and Sportsman received $15 each. Yet to win a race, Outbound benefited from a seven pound weight allowance entering at 111 pounds. Critics believed he could not win even if he carried only ninety pounds. Le Premier was inconsistently fast and not capable of the distance, it being a quarter of a mile beyond his capabilities, and Sportsman was just out-classed. The last heavyweight at 121 pounds, Bryant's Come-to-Taw was not rated in these pools. His entrance presented a puzzle to reporters, for they knew he could not make the pace, and that in laying off it, he most certainly would be outrun at the finish. They did not know that this was part of Bryant's plan. Come-to-Taw was to pace Knott through the mile, and then Knott was expected to overtake him for the victory.

The horses well-campaigned, more fit, mature, and experienced, the American Derby was believed a better test of the country's crack three-year-olds than the Kentucky Derby. A win for Spokane might make him a phenomenal three-time winner. Proctor Knott risked the titles of equine champion or duffer depending on his finish, and Don Jose could become a great runner or a short horse. Mighty reputations were made or broken in less than three minutes.

Proctor Knott was to be ridden by 'Dare Devil' Fitzpatrick, a rider of the Eastern circuit who had not had a Western mount since Montrose in the 1887 Kentucky Derby. Sam Bryant originally intended Jimmy McLaughlin be given the ride, but McLaughlin could not make the weight. Fitzpatrick, however, was equally rated and known for his determined riding and desperate finishes. Bryant made sure that Knott would be ridden for all he was worth.

A shrewd and calculating turfman, many thought Sam Bryant had purposely kept Proctor Knott from winning prior to Chicago in order that his goliath might go to the post without penalty. His confidence and his strategy to be proved this Derby day, Bryant was either a wise judge of horseflesh or an empty, boastful braggart.

An honest and masterly rider, Isaac Murphy was persistently in the American Derby winner's circle. In 1884, he rode the winner, Modesty. In 1885, it was Volante, and in 1886, aboard Silver Cloud, Murphy again stole the honors. Missing in 1887, he came back to win in 1888 atop the Emperor of Norfolk. Thus, the "colored Archer" was a four-of-five-tries winner. Once Again, the *Chicago Daily Tribune* said, was "fit to run for a Prince's realm."

Dan McCarty still searched for a worthy jockey to ride Sorrento. Taral, Duffy, and Stoval were possibilities. Duffy, once a renowned jockey, succumbed to a bad drinking habit, leaving Stoval and Taral in contention. Taral won the mount.

A jockey for J. B. Haggin, Winchell was engaged to ride Don Jose whose stable following scoffed at suggestions that their colt could not go the Derby distance, musing, "Wait and see."

Missourians esteemed Le Premier, the Kansas City colt. Wednesday past, he won the Kansas City Derby, and just previous to that, he claimed the Bankers' and Brokers' Stakes at St. Louis. Le Premier's owner retained Elkie, the jockey that had guided him to these victories.

Pike Barnes, spurned as a jockey by Sam Bryant after the Kentucky Derby, got the ride on Long Dance. Barnes' fee was an extravagant $1,000.

Issac Lewis was hired by Ike Labold who declared that he would start his filly, Retrieve, "Just to see how far the Derby candidates can best her."

Sportsman appeared very sore and unable to run at any speed. Outbound was also rumored as out of it.

Public performance showed Spokane a grand horse. He had felt his rival's speed and found it wanting. Noted as providing exciting finishes with his come-from-behind attitude, John Rodegap admitted, "Spokane has to be urged."

In Lexington, Mr. James Murphy, a local trainer, compared Spokane to his successful 1886 Kentucky Derby charge, Ben Ali, and in Louisville fans hurried to Chicago to back Proctor Knott one more time. These last included: Mr. and Mrs. Murray Kellar, Chancery Marshal Motz, William M. Collins, Charles Godshaw, Colonel John H. Whallen, Wilbur F. Adkins, August Strauss, George Herbert, Ike Abrams, Dowling Woods, Henry Johnson, and Walter Kerr. Those that could not otherwise attend crowded into the four Louisville pool rooms and anxiously awaited news of the soon-to-be-run Sixth American Derby.

Scheduled to begin promptly at 2:30, the Chicago races were timed by a large clock opposite the judges' stand, a clock that started and stopped by electricity.

Heavy betting kept forty bookmakers busy, a great number when compared to the thirteen present at the Kentucky Derby. Fifty applications for bookstands were received, but space limited the number allowed. Drawings were held to determine the forty. Those acquiring stands were charged $95 a day for the privilege and were required to purchase admission tickets for themselves and their employees.

James Murphy of Chicago wagered $2,500 to $1,000 against Spokane and gave $2,000 to $1,000 against Don Jose.

In the wild West that was Spokane's home, racing patrons near Anaconda, Montana, witnessed a shoot out. Scalp Perry, a prospector, ended a long-standing feud with William McCoy. The assassin then mounted his horse and escaped into the mountains, pursued by a sheriff's posse.

Rosy rays, the gifted light of a golden sun, brushed Chicago's Washington Park track. Exciting futures awaited fulfillment. Derby day dawned. □

15 Crowds, Wagers, And Tension

"It was a day of astonishing features — the immensity of the crowd; the elegance; the variety; the number of the equipages; the fierceness of the struggle to reach bookmakers' stands and the enormous sums wagered on the contest; the closeness and gameness of the great race from start to finish; the enthusiasm that greeted the winner and his rider — all were parts of a whole the like of which has never before been seen on any race track."
Chicago Sunday Tribune: June 23, 1889.

A coach sounded its horn in front of the Leland Hotel impatiently summoning the guests to get aboard. "Yo ho-o-o-o, ho, ho, ho, ho, ho-o-o-o!" It called. The Washington Park colors fluttered from the whip stock as, with a flourish, Derby Day was inaugurated.

Like the swirls of water at a mighty river's confluence, so were the colorful crowds that flowed into line along Michigan Avenue. By 1:15, these brightly-bedecked patrons were eagerly off for a day of racing thrills.

From Jackson Street to Thirty-ninth, every species of vehicle joined the procession southward. Tramping hooves, hooting horns, beribboned horses, and a garden of parasols rolled onward. Statuesque horses mounted by park policemen stood with staring eyes, seemingly undaunted by the steady pressure of the masses that slowly moved through the club gates.

Five well-defined lines of vehicles approached. One had to wonder where on earth so many rigs came from, and what the rest of the world was finding to ride in.

One gentleman on the Club House veranda observed, "I'll take back all the harsh words I have used about the liveryman. I started out Tuesday to engage a swell rig for today, and I think I telephoned every stable of any size in town. I wanted a Victoria, and I found just one in all Chicago that was not engaged. It wasn't what you would call a first class rig, and the liveryman's figure was $20. I thought it was a game of 'bluff,' but now I'll take it all back."

The variety of vehicles was remarkable: coaches, carriages, carts, suspension mail phaetons, rockaways, Victorias, landaus, broughams, surreys, road carts, T-carts, drags, elegant family carriages, light-running side bars, natty coupes, capricious hacks, humble cabs, and even bicycles. All shared the same objective, to reach the Derby grounds.

Inside the gates, ninety-seven stalls accommodated the rigs of private members while outside, the quest for standing space filled rude sheds and vacant lots. From 3,300 to 3,950 vehicles sought asylum.

First to arrive at the Club House was the coach of Mr. Charles Swartz driven by four horses: two bays in front, a black and gray behind. With him were Mrs. Ed Norton, Miss King, Mrs. Laura Williams, Mr. Munro, Mr. Fred Keep, Mr. Chatfield, Mr. and Mrs. Arthur Caton, and Miss Kellogg.

Mrs. Caton was attired in a gray India silk gown trimmed with white. Her costume was accented by a black straw hat and a black fur cape. Miss Kellogg, like many other fine ladies, wore black lace and net topped by a black lace hat.

Pulling up in style, the Swartz' Coachman 'Arry Simmons and Groom 'Enry Price dropped from the rear step with the last blast of the bugle and rushed to the heads of the brown leaders, checking them with the chestnut and gray wheelers. Assisted by the gentlemen, the ladies alighted.

Next, came the four-in-hand of Mr. Hobart C. Taylor, a fine rig with a gleaming black body trimmed with brilliant yellow. Miss George Wadsworth, Miss McElroy, Mr. Horace White of Syracuse, Mr. C.D. Lathrop, Mr. T.A. Marsh, Mr. and Mrs. Reginald DeKoven, and Miss Houghtaling were aboard. All of the ladies wore yellow roses coordinating with their coach. Mrs. DeKoven, attired in French costume, wore blue and white with a tulle hat. Her companion, Mrs. Houghtaling's hat was trimmed with real violets.

Mr. R.H. McCormick's black and red coach drawn by four closely matched strawberry roans next arrived, and its occupants disembarked. Mrs. McCormick was elegant in blue and black silk complete with a black beaded wrap.

In addition to the club house elite, the grandstand held sixty-eight private boxes which ran the length of the second story. These boxes each comfortably held half a dozen people, and afforded an ample view of the races from start to finish.

Unlike Kentucky, the weather was cool and cloudy, almost threatening. But like Kentucky, the who's who of society were present. Lists of the notables, their manner of dress, and descriptions of their vehicles occupied fully six columns of the *Chicago Sunday Tribune*. Part of the charm of Derby Day was being seen and being properly recognized as having attended. It was a social happening, and it was news.

By 2:30, the Washington Park grandstand was packed to the roof. Vendors of peanuts and chewing-gum wove their way through the pressing throngs conducting a vigorous trade. Frantic hands grabbed for programs, and the lawn appeared "like flypaper covered with struggling victims in Derby hats."

The bell for the first race rang. Time watches were opened, and eyes quickened in search of horses entering the track. The band played. Another "Clang! Clang!" brought every man to his feet. The race was on.

A red-faced policeman shouted, "Sit down there! Sit Down! Down in front!"

"Rah! Ah-h-Nh-h-O-o-o-h. Bad Start!" The assemblage sank to their seats.

The electric current of excitement surged again as "There they go!" was heard once more.

Shouting themselves hoarse and tossing their hats into the air, the crowd cheered the winner home. Robin Hood and Marchma fought gamely to the line. The favorite, Marchma, returned to the stable "covered with glory and perspiration."

Next, Penn P. easily beat his field. The wild hysteria diminished slightly. Spirits were saved for the featured race, the American Derby, third on the five-race programme.

Variously estimated at between 50,000 and 75,000, these crowd figures were conservatively trimmed to 30,000 for official reporting purposes. Washington Park printed 23,000 tickets for Derby Day and sold an additional 3,000 stubs. Of eight hundred club members, few missed. Most brought their families and friends as well, bringing club attendance to between 3,000 and 4,000 fans. Owners, stablemen, and complimentary ticket holders attended, as did 5,000 people transported in sixty carloads of the Illinois Central Railroad. Fully 4,000 vehicles of all description arrived, and cable cars brought the remainder of the enormous crowd to the grounds.

In the betting quarters, men fought to risk their dollars. One frequent, but conservative better stated, 'I am sound of body and mind, of average size, and considered a good man in a catch-as-catch-can. I am not deficient in nerve and not over timid. I have shared in the struggle of many a hard fought football field, and I have done my share in some pretty lively college rushes.

"But I never had just such an experience...As soon as the second race was run I entered the betting quarters intending to place $10 on Once Again. I got along nicely for the first fifty feet. Everybody was going the same way. Then it began to get a trifle close. A good many men and some pretty stocky fellows, too, began to get frightened and turn back. This made matters worse. I would have followed suit except that I was betting for a lady and did not like to acknowledge that I lacked the physical power to place her money. About this time, I quit fooling and settled down to business. I got within five feet of a bookmaker's stall. Then I discovered that I could not get my hand down to my watch pocket for my money. Finally, I did. Then I could not get elbow room to open my roll of bills. At last I did. Then I could not get my hand above my head. Before I did get one arm out I had been carried past three stalls. I did at last get my money into a bookmaker's hands. He refused any bet less than $5 with scorn. I suppose I saw $5,000 held in the air within a radius of twenty feet of me by frantic men, who could not get within arm's length. Everybody was shouting. Many were cursing. Not a few cried out in pain and alarm. One man near me yelled that his leg was being broken. Men warned each other not to lose their footing. To have fallen would have meant certain death. There would have been blows struck had there been room to strike.

"Having placed my money the next thing was to get out. I tried it for fifteen minutes and I made no progress. At length I found myself shoulder to shoulder with four other men in the same fix. We compared notes. Then we united forces. Probably some of the men in our immediate vicinity did not like our method of getting out, but we got out. Our united force accomplished what none of us singly had been able to do. When I reached the open air I was as exhausted as a wrestler after a fall, bathed in perspiration, and sore from the pressure. The cigars in my vest pocket were broken in pieces and the crystal of my hunting-case gold watch was shattered."

In Louisville, pool rooms were comfortably crowded as early as ten o'clock in the morning. At four exchanges: the Turf Exchange, Newmarket, Brown and Co., and Enright and Co., auctioneers were busy placing money for the betters. As the hours passed, these rooms became jammed. Only one man in a hundred backed Spokane.

Post time neared. Of the eleven presumed starters, four were scratched: Outbound, Come-to-Taw, Sportsman, and Le Premier. This left seven horses in competition: Don Jose, Long Dance, Once Again, Proctor Knott, Retrieve, Spokane, and Sorrento.

Money flowed in from the Northwest. Spokane was a heavy favorite at 6 to 5, Proctor Knott was 2 to 1; Don Jose 9 to 2; Once Again 7 to 1; and Sorrento 6 to 1. Long shots were Retrieve at 25 to 1 and Long Dance at 40 to 1.

Sam Bryant heavily backed his horse. Not a man who handled his money recklessly or even liberally, he placed $200 on Proctor Knott, as much as Bryant was ever known to wager at one time. His cheerful attitude and confident backing was communicated to the crowd.

August Strauss, President of the Courier-Journal Job Printing Company of Louisville, bet heavily on Proctor Knott. So too, did Mr. Harris, Tony Carroll, Steve Roberts, Henry Baxter, James B. Love, and C. B. Stuart. The combined trust of these men equalled approximately $24,500.

Privately, Bryant expressed some doubt. "My horse is not only poor in flesh, but short in preparation. He will fall away beaten at the head of the stretch, I expect. Had the track been heavy, I should have started Come-to-Taw, too, for he is as good a horse as anybody has when the going is bad. In my opinion, the fight to the finish will lie between Once Again and Don Jose."

Preliminary practice runs were conducted. Proctor Knott and Spokane took theirs at the same time. Both were blanketed.

Proctor Knott fans were hopeful when they witnessed the return of the elastic stride and magnificent sweep as Knott worked through the stretch, but little of the beloved gelding was visible save his head and feet.

Spokane was led in front of the multitude arrayed in his kingly attire of silk plush and gold. Admiring citizens of Spokane Falls distributed circulars promoting their community. Astutely conducting business prior to the race, they took no chances. Spokane might lose his crown, but Spokane Falls would not lose its opportunity. Wild cheering attended the champion's appearance. However, critically watched, Spokane's work was not judged as impressive as his attire.

A clanging bell called the racers onto the track. First to appear was Sorrento with Taral up. He was greeted by a few stray cheers.

Next, were the game chicken colors sported by Fitzpatrick on Proctor Knott. The now customary ovation welcomed Knott's honored presence, but it was quickly followed by exclamations of dismay. Once visible, the chestnut sides revealed ribs and a bony anatomy. Proctor Knott was painfully light in flesh and looked badly touched up. Upon seeing him with Sam Bryant at his head, looking anxious but hopeful, Knott's backers immediately desired to hedge their bets.

One disgusted Kentuckian emotionally announced, "D__m that Bryant, anyhow...He promised not to 'try' that horse after leaving Louisville, but I'll bet any kind of odds that he's done a hard mile and a half every morning since he's been here."

Proctor Knott was followed onto the track by Long Dance ridden by Barnes and Don Jose with Winchell up. The Labold Brothers' colors of canary and purple next came into view. Retrieve with Lewis on board looked fit and queenly. Isaac Murphy received well-earned applause when he rode Once Again beyond the gate.

Orange and blue silks shimmered. Thomas Kiley grinned confidently. John Rodegap and Noah Armstrong gazed proudly. Spokane loped passed the cheering thousands to the post. ☐

16 Third Time Charm

The racing programs were sold out, vendors' merchandise exhausted. Spectators grasped their hats. An expectant policeman braced himself against a pillar. Small boys clung desperately to tall pickets, and diligent guards secured the track. On the club house grounds, the shifting kaleidoscope of color was held imprisoned by the moment.

"Clang! Clang!"

"The Derby! The Derby! Hurrah!"

Like delicate flowers at dusk, parasols withdrew into themselves, as glasses leveled onto the starters for the great American Derby.

At four o'clock on Saturday, June 22, 1889, the bugle summoned the flyers for the Sixth American Derby to the post. On the backstretch in front of Starter James G. Sheridan's box, the horses took their positions. From his vantage point, only thirty yards from the half mile post, Mr. Sheridan saw that Proctor Knott was fighting to be free in spite of Fitzpatrick's valiant efforts.

One of Knott's backers remarked, "He's rank today."

Suddenly, the field was away. As they streamed past Sheridan's box, it appeared to onlookers a fair start.

"They're off! They're off!" cried the crowd.

Sheridan did not tap the drum. The signal flag remained up. A murmur of surprise and disappointment rolled across the grandstand. Exclamations of protest sounded.

"That was a good start!" "Why didn't he send them off!"

Proctor Knott was still visible around the upper turn struggling for his head. Along with Long Dance, he refused to be pulled up readily.

Upon finally being returned to the post, the Futurity winner persisted in his desire to be off. Foam appeared starkly white against the sweat-darkened hide of the massive chest. Impossible to control at the front,

Proctor Knott was led thirty yards to the rear.

Calmed for now, the racers waited. A second break was made, and spoiled. McCarty's Sorrento sulked. Maddened by the previous false start, he refused to move.

Proctor Knott, a veritable devil, was again running away. His backers were frustrated.

"There he goes, running his race at the post. He'll beat himself."

Jockeys cursed their neighbors, and horses stamped defiantly. Assembled for a third time, the racers broke. Once more, Sorrento stood. Surprisingly, Proctor Knott took on a congenial attitude as he returned after advancing only a short distance. But he snorted and tossed his head, as he was brought to the rear for the recall. Spokane, previously a ready angel awaiting his master's call, began to chomp his bit and hump his back in vigorous protest. Nostrils flared, red with anticipation.

Fully fifteen minutes since the first call to the post, the anxious Derby warriors assembled for the fourth time. Sorrento was cajoled into moving, and Proctor Knott's head was loosed. The jockeys scrambled for position. Fairly bunched at last, the starter's drum tapped, and the flag was lowered. A hearty cheer burst from the multitude.

First to emerge was Once Again. Having stood quietly through the torture of the post, he led the party confidently. Lapping Once Again was Don Jose. The pack was about one hundred and fifty yards behind. Murphy eased Once Again back.

Halfway around the upper turn, Proctor Knott found the window opened by Once Again, and he instantly seized a two-length lead. The crowd enthusiastically applauded this move.

Following and running abreast were Don Jose, Long Dance, and Retrieve. Sorrento, under Taral's able hand, was content with fifth position on the outside. Kiley, in last position, snugly held the favorite and dropped two lengths.

Before the first quarter was complete, Proctor Knott let loose more of his giant strides, and the gap between his rivals and himself was four open lengths.

From the lawn, shouts arose.

"They'll never catch him."

By the three-quarter mark, Knott was well in front. Long Dance and Retrieve were next and running nearly together. Once Again attempted to move around them on the outside. Behind these was Sorrento by half a length. The mountain colt trailed.

Murphy and Kiley tightly restrained their mounts, saving them to later challenge Proctor Knott. Thus rated, Spokane exercised a "long stealing stride that was the perfection of horse in motion."

Down the homestretch and swinging into the second quarter, the thundering hooves pounded. In an effort to conserve the bold and blaze-faced Knott, Fitzpatrick steadily reined him in, effectively reducing the gelding's lead to two lengths. Fitzpatrick was "waiting in front" as Bryant had ordered.

The great Isaac Murphy, seeing Proctor Knott slacking the pace, took a strong wrap on Once Again dropping him one length behind the second division, a solid and comfortable fifth place.

Thomas Kiley noticed the slowing, and he too, dropped back a length. The pride of Spokane Falls continued his run in last position.

Jockeys Barnes, Lewis, and Winchell still abreast bravely fought to hold their positions. Taral aboard Sorrento, the full brother of the 1887 American Derby winner, moved forward along the inside rail.

As the first half was completed, Sorrento assumed second place. Knott, in the winning fashion of old, held the lead by two lengths as he passed the stands for the first time. "Dare Devil Fitz" had the giant in hand. Knott's head was well up. When the popular colt flashed passed the grandstand, the spectators cheered wildly.

"He's got a man on him today!"

"He will win in a canter!"

"Look at a race horse, boys!"

Trailing Sorrento by half a length were the threesome of Long Dance, Retrieve, and Don Jose. Behind these, Murphy held Once Again, and yet another length to the rear was Spokane. Both Murphy and Kiley were perched like statues atop their mounts. Montana's hope trailed by a full four lengths, and Kiley made no effort to advance his position.

In the third quarter, Winchell pulled in Don Jose, as did Lewis on Retrieve. Barnes continued to push Long Dance, claiming the third position.

The horses were halfway through the turn. Once Again was running smoothly along the rail seemingly alone, but a quick glance to the right by Murphy revealed Spokane dangerously near. Kiley decided to let the copper king out a notch.

Proctor Knott completed the turn still ahead, but Sorrento was pressing, and Long Dance was only a length behind him. The rest of the field followed. Don Jose and Retrieve were next by a length, Once Again and Spokane by two.

Undaunted, Fitzpatrick continued Knott's "big gallop," increasing his advantage another length. Invincible once more, the old Proctor Knott of Futurity fame romped easily into the backstretch.

Sorrento, laboring from his unsuccessful effort to catch Knott, was working to stay ahead of Long Dance. Quick to notice that Knott had increased the pace, Murphy on Once Again and Kiley aboard Spokane closed rapidly on Don Jose and Retrieve. Once Again chose the inside path. Spokane got around on the outside.

When Murphy, the "brown Archer," appeared on the rail, the blacks

Spokane winning the American Derby. Front page news in the Chicago Sunday Tribune, *June 23, 1889*

present screamed with delight. Their hero might well win the American Derby for a remarkable fifth time.

From the Chicago grandstand, Spokane was spotted, and from the spirit world, energy flowed.

"There goes Kiley!"

Clustered at the mile mark, Long Dance, Retrieve, Don Jose, Once Again, and Spokane hurried to the finish. Midway through the backstretch, Murphy caught the tiring second place, Sorrento. Don Jose dropped back and was hopelessly boxed.

On the outside, Spokane took on the sleek filly, Retrieve. Proctor Knott's once mighty lead shrank to only one length.

In the upper turn for the second and last time, the field closed on the magnificent Knott.

"They're going to him!"

"They've got him!"

But the son of Luke Blackburn was not finished. From deep within his goliath frame, he tapped a powerful reserve. When Once Again challenged him, Proctor Knott fought him head for head. The pair drew away from the others.

Only a brief spurt, the valiant effort failed almost as soon as it was born. Near the end of the turn, the leaders fell back.

Swiftly, Sorrento, Retrieve, and Spokane battled to the front. Don Jose challenged.

Thomas Kiley reached for his whip.

Onlookers yelled, "He's a loafer."

"He's got to be driven."

Fiction transcended time and space. Tragedy inspired promise, response to a brave chief's prayer.

The faintest murmur stirred upon the breeze. There appeared to be some life emerging from the lifeless forms... Amotkan spoke, "Do not lose heart brave Chief Tilcoax. This is a spirit horse..."

Long Dance was having difficulty. Once Again had been "stalled off," and Proctor Knott had "shot his bolt." Spokane had a chance for victory, but so did Sorrento, Don Jose, and Retrieve.

The California entry, Sorrento, led by a scant neck. Retrieve was next, a neck in front of Spokane. She ran well, and momentarily it appeared that the Sixth American Derby might well crown a queen.

Whips beat a cruel tattoo upon the flanks of Sorrento and Spokane, Taral and Kiley driving their mounts stubbornly onward.

One old turfman upon seeing Spokane as he entered the final quarter said sadly, "He's beaten beyond recovery. If ever I saw a beaten horse there's one."

Kiley would not let Spokane accept defeat. Sorrento capitulated, but Retrieve hung on.

"Whips were flying on fire when they had only a furlong to go."

The pace grew hotter. Long Dance was the first to yield. Next was Don Jose. Taral mercilessly urged Sorrento, and gamely the colt responded. Retrieve was not out of it, but she was obviously wearing down. At last, the stouter Spokane, his mountain lungs expanded to their limit, overcame the courageous filly. With fame and glory only one hundred yards away, Spokane drew clear.

Or did he? Sorrento swung into second position and began a steady advance on the favorite.

Desperately Kiley gathered his chestnut stallion and steered him toward the inner rail, lashing Spokane at every stride.

Memory sought reality.

One day he (the spirit horse) will return with the speed, the endurance, and the pluck of all the horses dead on the battlefield. He will enter into the body of a colt, and will go forth to conquer all the horses of the earth.

Infused with extraordinary power, Spokane launched one last heart-rending effort. Straightened by Kiley, Spokane plunged home, the winner by a clever length.

Hats flew into the air as men leaped to their feet; some in uncontrollable exultation jumped the railing. Others turned pale. White lips shut tightly. Strong efforts were made at self control as the unbelievable result became official.

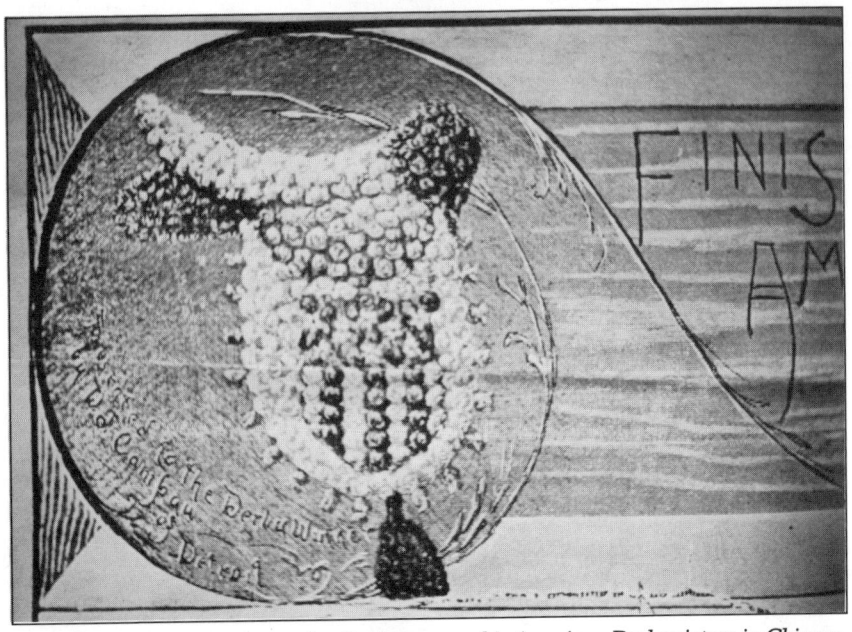

The *"Saddle of Roses"* presented to Spokane upon his American Derby victory in Chicago. It was the gift of D.J. Champau, editor of the *Chicago Horseman.*

One man commented, "The owner of that horse is a good deal richer than he was a half hour ago."

The response came, "Twenty thousand dollars wouldn't touch him."

Sorrento was second, and Retrieve third. Next was Don Jose followed by Long Dance. The once unbeatable Proctor Knott, disgraced, humbled, and abused, was last. Bryant hastily recovered the exhausted giant and headed for the stables.

The weary Spokane entered the paddock area, his head drooped, sweat glistened across his back, and his step was slow. The gates closed, but the crowd surged after him, demanding his return. They wished to again see the David that had slain the Kentucky Goliath.

What transpired next was a tribute the like of which had never before been witnessed on any race track. Deafening cheers heralded the return of Spokane. Looking miraculously refreshed and renewed, Spokane emerged from the paddock gates. Victory blessed him, and as a brilliant sun broke through the clouds, Spokane took his triumphal march. A band played, and beneath a king's coat of blue and gold, Spokane arched his proud neck; his handsome hooves danced. Officials of Washington Park placed a saddle of yellow roses, the gift of D. J. Campau of Detroit, upon his back.

An Indian chief crossed peacefully on to the final hunting ground, his satisfied spirit at rest.

"The losses of your people will be redeemed in his name, Spokane, Child of the Sun." □

17 Horse For All Regions

On the day after the American Derby, Noah Armstrong's daughter, Emma, lovingly clipped an article from the *Helena Independent*. Back in Montana, she eagerly clung to every bit of information sent from the East, and this particular article deserved preservation in her treasured scrapbook. It read:

"The race is run, and Spokane has won. It would be superfluous to add anything to the merit of Montana's great colt. Spokane is now conceded the greatest piece of horseflesh on the continent; he has accomplished what no other animal has done - won in succession three of the greatest honors of the American turf and against the strongest fields a horse was ever pitted. The successes are more to Montana than could ever have been dreamed of. All eyes are now turned this way and in the future any one who does not know where Spokane is from will be far behind the times...dispatches state that the Washington Park track was four seconds slow; it thus seems Spokane has made another best Derby record, his time being 2:41 1/2...Nothing but the American 'Darby' was talked of yesterday, and the news being delayed until rather late, the suspense grew greater. The crowd around the bulletin boards surpassed that at the time of the running of the Clark Stakes, and the cheering that followed when the welcome news flashed over the wires caused a scene of enthusiasm rarely witnessed. Helena wins a barrel of money and last night a carmine hue was noticeable throughout the city. The croakers who said Spokane would lose, and they are few, are not to be found.

"The success of Spokane only further verifies the prediction of Montana horse breeders, who have invested their fortunes in this business, that Montana has the climate and grass to make the speediest horseflesh in the world. Horse racing is a national sport and the interest increases yearly. The result is that Montana horseflesh will be at a premium in the future, and the Bunch Grass State will lead the world, as Spokane is now king of the turf."

One can imagine Emma slowly shutting her book, silently relishing the glory of the moment.

Cecil Wetmore, Spokane's Montana trainer, was especially pleased by the fiery stallion's astonishing finish, coming from last place to win. He bragged, "That is the way Spokane loves to run. It makes this horse more exciting to watch than any other horse I know."

Pride was showing in Chicago, too. The *Chicago Daily Tribune* began its account of June 23: "It's an Illinois Day. An Illinois bred colt wins the great Illinois race. An Illinois jockey pilots him to victory. Illinois money makes him favorite over a field representing the proudest blood of the turf from California to the Gulf and to the Atlantic Coast.

"Thirty thousand loyal Illinoians see horse and rider pass under the wire, and 30,000 ecstatic sons and daughters of the Prairie State raise such a shout of exultation as only such a scene and hour and deed can call forth.

"It was a day of days even for the great Northwest and Chicago. There have been American Derby days before this, but none like it. Illinois men said there had never been anything like it in Chicago. Californians, Kentuckians, and New Yorkers admitted that it was unique. Men who had been on every race course on the civilized globe said they had never seen its equal."

So eager were the citizens of Illinois for ownership of Spokane that one inventive reporter there even challenged Montana as Spokane's place of birth. The admittedly fanciful account tells of how Armstrong obtained the colt, Spokane, from General Rowett, proprietor of The Meadows near Carlinville, Illinois. It stated: "Two years ago Armstrong purchased...a yearling Thoroughbred...When General Rowett saw the newly foaled colt, he declared the youngster must be shot. He was so puny and out of proportion that it would not pay to raise him...However, when Mr. Armstrong priced this weakling among other racers, its owner thought himself well rid of a cast-off for $250. Armstrong shipped the colt to his Montana farm..."

Ella Rowett, wife of the late General Rowett wrote later to dispel the confusion. Addressing her letter to the editor of the *Chicago Horseman*, she wrote: "The late General Rowett owned both the sire and dam of Spokane. Mr. Armstrong purchased Grey Cloud, full brother of Spokane when a yearling. He was so well pleased with his running when it came a two-year-old that he constituted a trust. He came to the farm and purchased Interpose when in foal to Hyder Ali. She was shipped to Montana that fall, 1885, and in the spring foaled the colt which was afterward named Spokane. I have been amused at the varied accounts of the history of the colt, but realizing that life isn't worth living without the price of variety, I give the newspaper correspondents the credit of diversity..."

Mrs. Rowett then described the Salt Lake City account attributing Spokane's success to the ozone of the mountains as "a fine theory," but emphasized the fact that "...he crossed the Rockies when a two-year-old and has not been back since. With all due credit to the ozone of the mountains and to the limestone of the bluegrass of other states, yet when a fast horse is wanted to beat the record, Illinois comes to the front as the banner state as she has for everything great and good."

In Kentucky, the *Louisville Courier-Journal* that once made reference to "the despised Montana colt," suddenly proclaimed him a local good fellow: "Kentuckians and Tennesseeans have been faithful to Proctor Knott, and their empty pockets attest the depth of the devotion they have lavished upon the big chestnut gelding, but it is now time for them to gracefully acknowledge the superiority of the Montana colt, since it has been proven in three exciting duels of speed. If our representative had to be beaten, we prefer that Spokane should have been the winner since he is half a Kentuckian himself, for, though not born of Kentucky soil, he is of pure Kentucky blood and dates his descent from the Bluegrass."

This article continued, "It is a pity that Spokane is not entered in any of the great Eastern Stakes, where he could meet the blue bloods of the New York racing stables. Although carrying extra weights, the ease with which he ran away from the pride of Kentucky and California at Chicago proves that he is not likely to meet a dangerous competitor on either side of the Alleghenies."

Spokane Falls, Washington Territory, earned both proprietary and relocation rights. Their rich blanket drew attention. A Louisville report erroneously printed that it was the extravagant gift of the citizens of "Spokane Falls, Montana."

One pictorial entitled, "Tale of the Turf", depicted in cartoon form, "The Sporting Enthusiast Who Once Had An Idea That Proctor Knott Was Invincible." The humorous series first showed a confident backer nattily dressed standing in front of a board bearing Proctor Knott's name. In the next picture, the better was shown scratching his head as he read the incredible news, "Proctor Knott: Kentucky Derby: Lost." In the third drawing, the gentleman was frowning, his hands sunk deeply into his pockets, and the board telling the sad story, "Proctor Knott: Clark Stakes: Lost." Finally, the frustrated Proctor Knott backer, in a flurry of exclamations, was pictured with his back to the board; his once-fine suit, now shabby; and both hands raised to his head, as his feet hastened away from the devastating news, "Proctor Knott: Chicago Derby: Lost."

Over a million dollars was reported to have exchanged hands during the American Derby. The Louisville pool rooms were accused of making a killing. When Joe Burt announced, "Spokane first past the post," the backers of the "three-time winner," gave a shout, but the greater number present, being Proctor Knott supporters, were silent. Only two "good winners" could be named in Louisville: Emil Bourlier, who bought the first pool at the Turf Exchange for $350 in for $800, and Eli Marks, who won $1,300 from the New Market Exchange.

Interviews with the various owners and jockeys occupied columns. Every aspect of the unbelievable race became instant news.

Thomas Kiley, acting as if he had done nothing unusual, responded to one reporter's questions as he weighed in following the great race. When asked what he thought of the colt, Kiley replied, "O, I reckon the colt's all right. He got there. He seems to be good enough. He won the Kentucky Derby, and the Clark Stakes, and the American Derby - I guess he'll do."

Asked if Spokane was hard to ride, Kiley without hesitation answered, "O no; he rides all right."

To the inquiry about his backing Spokane at betting stands, Kiley said, "Yes; I had a dollar or so laid." But of his winnings, Kiley only commented, "Not much."

Noah Armstrong attempted to clarify a question concerning the actual ownership of Spokane that arose out of his partnership with William Hundley in the operation of the Montana Stable. Armstrong emphasized that the partnership applied only to the stable, not to the individual horses of that stable. Hence, Noah Armstrong was the sole owner of Spokane, but the winnings earned were the joint property of the Montana Stable and as such were subject to division.

Mr. Armstrong also revealed that Spokane was badly handled as a two-year-old: "I don't know anything about handling a horse, but I dismissed the trainer and took hold of the colt myself, and he's been doing reasonably well this year."

As to the worth of the Derby, Armstrong gave it to be about $17,000, but to the question of his backing Spokane on the outside, Noah responded, "A little; not much. I had about $600 or $700 on him." He attested the odds at "eight to five" and his winnings, "close to $3,000 on the side."

To a rumor that Kiley would receive $5,000 and a Montana Thoroughbred for winning the Derby, Noah retorted, "No, there is no truth in that story. Kiley is well paid for his riding, and he won about $5,000 in bets he made on the horse sometime ago. Kiley owns a stable of race horses himself. He has had six or seven horses at the West Side track this season."

Was Kiley a regular employee? "I have the call on him when I want a heavyweight rider; I can't put him up on light mounts," Armstrong commented.

As to future engagements for Spokane, Noah stated, "I don't remember exactly what they are. He is entered for several stakes at Washington Park, including the Great Western Handicap, and he is entered for races in Westchester."

On Spokane's value, Noah firmly stated, "I don't care to sell him; I'm in the business of raising horses, and there is no reason why I should part with him." Pressed to name a price, Noah made it high. "Not less than $50,000," concluding, "He's a pretty good horse, you know."

The Chicago Mutuels on Spokane paid $13.60 to win and $10 to place. Sorrento's second place earned his backers, $18.40.

Excuses for Sorrento's loss were sought. Jockey Fred Taral, only twelve years old and already possessing five years of riding experience, offered only one reason, "Spokane got in first."

Wearing the customary white hat and a profusion of watch chain, Dan McCarty, Sorrento's owner, did not lose much. He had wisely backed his horse to place, but he said, "If he had come in first I'd have cleaned up $80,000. He's the best animal of the bunch and will be heard from later."

Taral, listening, added, "My mount sulked in the backstretch, and if the wire had been 100 yards farther away I believe I'd have landed the winner. I started second, dropped back to fourth at the first quarter, to sixth at the half, and then began closing up. I gained right along up to the backstretch, where I barely held my own, but picked up again as I came down the homestretch. The sulkiness of my mount in the backstretch settled it, but I'd have won, nevertheless, had the wire been a little farther away. Sorrento is a good one and will be heard from again."

That McCarty was satisfied was evident in a grin that competed with his watch chain for attention. He eyed his chestnut colt with "a look of pride that bespoke the truth of his utterance, 'I didn't lose anything.' "

Sam Bryant did lose something, and he knew it.

Upon dismounting, Fitzpatrick declared emphatically, "That is the worst cur I ever threw a leg over."

Uttering no word of reply, Sam Bryant's face alone reflected the intense inner anger and humiliation that was present. His countenance was "flushed to a degree that suggested danger of apoplexy." In spite of his crushed hopes, the owner slipped his hand gently and affectionately along the heaving and bleeding sides of his gelding, Proctor Knott, the horse that had so often disappointed him. The exhausted animal stood with drooping head and quivering limbs. Stoically, Bryant called his rider, "Come along, Johnny." Fitzpatrick came, though he bore a look that mirrored despair so complete as to be comical. The threesome, trailing, made their way to the stable. Bryant had no cause to celebrate, and his naturally boastful nature was quieted by the outcome.

Hard luck seemed Sam Bryant's fate of late, and some suggested its severity posed a danger to his nervous equilibrium. His filly, Charlotte Cushman, the sister of Proctor Knott for whom he had genuine hopes of repeating his triumph in the Futurity Stakes, and who had shown marvelous speed, was broken down. A ringbone had thrown her out of training. Benedict was dead, the result of accident, and Proctor Knott, only a month ago easily worth $25,000, had been beaten four times. Subsequently, his value was decreased to a level that was difficult to calculate. Sam Bryant, once prosperous, now suffered great adversity; a stable of sick horses that he could not run, and a mass of forfeits were pending that amounted to a small fortune.

Friends thought Bryant so rattled by his misfortune that he might ruin Proctor Knott for all time. Obsessed with getting Knott into shape, Bryant always had the great gelding on his mind. Acquaintances hinted, "He finds it hard to believe that the horse can run as fast at night as he did in the morning. To make certain he takes him out and tries him. Then the next morning he is again doubtful, and so to satisfy himself he sends Proctor another trial. It was said before the Kentucky Derby was run that Bryant would do an occasional trial at midnight, but that was hardly true. But, notwithstanding, the chestnut gelding, counting trials and his races, has run enough miles since the first of the season to have broken down an ordinary horse, and the only hope for him seems to be rest. Perhaps he can win sometime in the future, and perhaps he will continue to run second and last, but he certainly has a wonderful turn of speed, and if for nothing else than his ability, as a sprinter, deserves some care..."

Bob Tucker, a strong backer of Proctor Knott's, lost so much money through bad investment that he was forced to sell some of his stable and release the famed black jockey, Pike Barnes, from his employ. The lightweight's contract was snapped up by the Dwyers. It seemed that Sam Bryant's misfortune found company throughout Kentucky.

Seen on the Monday following the Derby, Sam was basking in the sun in front of Proctor Knott's Washington Park stall. He tried not to let his true feelings show. Interviewed, he said: "I have learned to take defeat philosophically. I have been in the horse business well on to forty years. When I was a lad I used to ride. Take my word for it, there is no use of borrowing trouble. When a man tackles training horses for a living he ought to make up his mind to one thing, there is not five minutes' difference between a rich man and a poor man and sometimes a d__m sight less."

Did Knott's loss surprise Bryant?

"As far as Proctor Knott is concerned, no."

Reminding reporters that he had doubted Knott would last through the stretch and that he was not as good a nag as he was when he started for the Derby, Bryant claimed, "He ran a good mile, and then stopped even more gradually than I thought. I am satisfied the horse had his speed, but not strength enough to carry it any further than he went.

"Proctor will go East, and very shortly now. He will have a long rest — just what he needs — and by the time Sheepshead Bay opens for its fall meeting, he will be in shape to beat anybody's horse. I'll make a killing with him before the season is over; just see if I don't. The whole trouble is Proctor Knott was dosed the night before the Clark Stakes was run. I've said so before, and I'll say it again, and when I get East I'll find out who did it as sure as I'm a living man.

"The horse was in a stall that had a window in the back, and when my back was turned somebody gave him a dose that deadened the horse all over. I knew that something had been done to Proctor when I saw him run in the Clark Stakes. I could not afford to take any chances, so I physicked the animal, and four hours afterward he began to grow better. But it will be some months yet before he's Proctor Knott again, and when he does round to, bet every dollar you've got in the world he beats any horse he meets."

Sam Bryant's loyalty and bravado, at least publicly, remained unshaken. However, it was rumored that "ninety-nine out of every 100 turfmen" considered Proctor Knott "a duffer of the first water."

All ifs aside, Spokane was the indisputable victor. His success was legendary from the outset. A poetic Chicago commentator wrote: "The medicine man of the Flathead tribe of Indians leaves his teepee every morning as the sun throws its first ray against the side of the Rocky Mountains, and in the crevices about the base of the big hills seeks and gathers a small, wild flower, from whose petals issues a rare fragrance. The plant is taken back into camp and dried, and from its leaves it is brewed into a tea that is regarded infallible in conquering all ills that attack the red skins or their ponies. From its constant use the Flatheads have become famous as examples of manly strength and health, and their ponies are the fleetest and stoutest.

"Noah Armstrong's horse farm lies in the Rocky Mountain divide between the Columbia and Missouri rivers in Montana, close to the Indian reservation . . . (Spokane) The raw-boned brute sniffed the air of the Rockies and was fed the wild flower of the Indians. He grew big and lusty, his sides expanded, his limbs became strong, and turning into his third year, the Illinois outcast (of General Rowett) was a thing of equine beauty. . .''

This imaginative author continued, speaking of Spokane's success, "Of no avail was the blue grass of Kentucky on which Once Again, Long Dance, and Retrieve had fed; to no purpose had Proctor Knott been carefully nourished on famous Tennessee bran; impure must have been the air in California's glorious climate for Don Jose and Sorrento, for Spokane cast from the prairies of Illinois and nursed to life by the dew of the Rockies and the little wild flower of the Flathead medicine man, raced away from them all, and became at once an equine marvel, winner of a triple event."

Spokane's recent Derby triumph was given fanciful detail, such as, "Spokane, came away under Kiley's upraised hand, but without tasting whip or spur, and won very easily over a full length."

Apparently enjoying his task, the author went on to describe, "When Spokane reached his stall he was almost mobbed by the Montana Stable's frenzied attendants who clung about his neck and would not allow him to rest until Trainer Rodegap had shouted himself hoarse. He was rubbed down and lightly fed, and as he went down to his stable, the stable boys gathered under the shed and told of the great horse's prowess. Shortly a tall, red-faced man, with a brown beard and hands thrust clumsily into his trouser pockets sauntered along the stable path. It was Sam Bryant on his way to his own stalls. As he passed the Montana stables, he was attracted by the laughter and loud talk, and turning in that direction, he saw a lusty darky place a big pot on the fire and fill it with small white leaves taken from a bag. It was the medicine man's lifegiver, and it was being prepared for Spokane's next meal. As the big darky stirred the steaming mass, his only, intelligible words were 'Spoke, my Spoke.' Sam Bryant sighed, a tear glistened in his eye, and he continued on his way to join Proctor Knott."

Controversy about the manner of the Derby's finish abounded. The following is taken from the *Spokesman Review* of July 7, 1889. "About the Spokane race: A Montana spectator who saw the finish talks about it. Wilke Sutherland of the *Rocky Mountain Husbandman* was in Helena yesterday on his way home from Chicago where he went to witness the great Derby. There has been some difference of opinion as to whether Kiley applied spur, or whip in finishing last Saturday's big event. Some reports are to the effect that he did, and others say he didn't. Mr. Sutherland was asked about this, and said the only time he saw Kiley draw his whip on Spokane was when he pulled away from Sorrento. The plucky little jockey had his whip ready again if necessary, but he never applied it. He kept one eye on Sorrento and the other on Retrieve, and gave Spokane his head. The latter had speed left for a run, but he was not called upon to make it. He passed the winning post fully 3/4 of a length ahead and did not finish a tired horse. 'The track is oval-shaped,' said Mr. Sutherland, 'and when above the turn coming into the long homestretch Spokane was pocketed by Proctor Knott and Sorrento. The pace was hot, and it would not do at this stage of the game for Kiley to turn out. He bided his time however, and just as the turn was reached Proctor faltered and was out of the race and Retrieve was then rushed to the front in an attempt to regain the position of Proctor Knott. Sorrento led for a short distance. Then the three; Retrieve,

Sorrento, and Spokane were on even terms, making a grand circle for the finish with Kiley once applying the catgut, and Spokane was out of reach.' "

In the same article, additional insight was offered into the nature of the business relationship between Colonel Hundley and Noah Armstrong. "Colonel Hundley guards Spokane with vigilance. Before the race he placed the guards before the grandstand and took no chances. On the other hand, Noah Armstrong might be seen in the Palmer House lobby. Mr. Armstrong is not anxious to sell Spokane but wishes to secure two colts by him. He says he has had many offers for the horse, but he is not at all interested. When asked if Spokane would start in the Twin City Derby, Mr. Armstrong said that he had not made up his mind, but it was fair to presume he will...Spokane is entered in the Montana Derby to run in Helena, but he is not expected to start."

From the Honorable Sam Warren, who also saw Spokane win, it was learned that Kiley was paid $1,000 for winning the race and that Mr. Armstrong felt confident of success before the start.

Spokane gave no evidence of lameness at the finish, and for the time being, the notion of the critics that a hard race would break him down was dispelled. "Though conceded to be clumsy when slow galloping or trotting, nothing adverse could be said of his racing stride." Appearing a trifle heavier in Chicago than in Kentucky, his coat was described in the *Louisville Courier-Journal* "as more roan than chestnut."

Everyone was interested to know when Spokane would race again. The *Louisville Courier-Journal* announced the Sheridan Stakes, a one and one quarter of a mile race, to be the next mountain colt's trial. It too was to be held at Washington Park in Chicago on Thursday, the Fourth of July. Because of his American Derby victory, Spokane was assigned a seven pound penalty. His company in that race was predicted to be much the same, and many hoped that Proctor Knott would recover soon enough to compete. A fierce rivalry existed that commanded satisfaction. But for the present, headlines proclaimed, "Proctor Not First," "Glorious Spokane," and "Spokane Forever." □

18 Fire To Flickering Flame

> Never was there more perfect racing weather. First, there was a warm sun for the especial benefit of the racers. Your Thoroughbred, be it known, loves the sunshine, and will not run his best unless he gets his fill. It was warm in the sun. Then the crowd likes to be in a cool place, especially when everybody is at the boiling point with excitement. So Lake Michigan furnished a breeze that was perfection itself. Neither rude enough to disarrange the silkiest trees nor chill the wearer of the daintiest summer costume, it came and went, cool with the freshness of the deep midlake springs and gentle as the playful little wavelets that flashed along the beach. So it was cool in the shade. Then there were clear skies to reassure the timid, and now and then a fleecy little cloud to temper the rays of old Sol when his gaze grew too fervid.
>
> *Chicago Tribune*, Friday, July 5, 1889.

Such was the Fourth of July at Washington Park, Chicago, on the day of the Sheridan Stakes when Spokane and Proctor Knott met for the fourth time.

Promised a program of grand sport and impelled to celebrate by the spirit of patriotism, approximately 22,500 people assembled. Unlike American Derby Day when the fashionable of Chicago society gathered, this day was a grandstand day. Family parties were numerous, and young men accompanied their best girls in regular holiday style. Picnic lunch baskets abounded, and the tantalizing smells of chicken, pickles, and cold tea bestowed fragrance upon the passing breeze. All seats were filled; the boxes were full; and even standing room was scarce.

On the grounds movement was possible, though not comfortable or easy. Not dependent on carriages, this crowd arrived in the everyday "grip car" and aboard the Illinois Central train. A good-natured group, crowding was not objected to. On the whole, they were easily pleased and bent on having a good time. Notably absent on this Independence Day was the small boy with his pesky firecracker, but in profusion were willing wagerers.

Three of every five men bet on Spokane to win the Sheridan Stakes, the remaining two would hear of nothing but Proctor Knott. "Bookies" took a long time to mark the odds, and one old turfman commented that it was the first time he had seen them afraid of a race and crowd. When the figures did finally appear, a wild scramble began which lasted until the horses were called from the paddock. Rushing to view the race, people hurried hastily into the stands.

To the winner, the Sheridan Stakes was valued at $5,350 by one account, $5,450 by another. It was contested by a field of seven: Spokane, Proctor Knott, Retrieve, Once Again, Heron, Glockner, and Beth Broeck. At 125 pounds, Spokane was the field's heavyweight. Once Again carried 123 pounds. The lightweight was Beth Broeck at 103 pounds, benefiting from a ten pound maiden allowance. Beth Broeck was ridden by Stoval, a popular jockey whose excellent riding at this Chicago meet had won for him many friends. Retrieve bore 118 pounds and was again ridden by Lewis. Kiley repeated on Spokane, and Isaac Murphy piloted Once Again. Proctor Knott at 115 pounds was under a new rider, Finnegan. Pike Barnes was up on Heron who carried 118 pounds to the post as did Glockner, the steed of jockey R. Williams.

Closing odds were 6 to 5 on Spokane, 8 to 5 on Proctor Knott, 15 to 1 each on Beth Broeck, Once Again, and Heron, and 20 to 1 on each of the others.

There was a strong tip out for Proctor Knott. A veteran trainer stated, "He is good today, and it will take a race horse to beat him."

Listed officially as "heavy," the track was mostly dry, but rough from the middle to the outside. Close to the inside rails the going was cuppy at all points. The backstretch and the upper turn were particularly wet on the surface and soft underneath.

As the racers came onto the track, Spokane with Kiley up was loudly cheered, but as before when Proctor Knott came into view, the crowd showed him their favor by unleashing a storm of applause that lasted until he was by the stand and up the stretch.

On the second break, the horses were away, being nearly in line when the flag fell. Hardly had the cry, "They're off!," subsided when Proctor Knott's white-blazed face appeared in front. Keeping him close company were: Heron, Spokane, Retrieve, and Beth Broeck. Glockner and

Once Again were running under restraint. Finishing the first quarter in 25 seconds, Knott pounded onward. Spokane was a slim second, only a shoulder in front of Heron, Retrieve, and Beth Broeck. The first half was completed in 51 1/2 seconds, and the giant Knott had opened a one and one half length lead over Spokane, his closest competitor. Spokane put a length between himself and the third place, Retrieve. Once Again was fourth and the others were already out of contention. The three-quarters were run in 1:17 1/2.

In the upper turn, Kiley let a link out on Spokane. The excited crowd cried, "See Kiley go up now!" Spokane began to close on the leader, just as Retrieve was closing on him. Halfway around, a regular Kentucky scream was heard that echoed from the lawn and betting quarters to the grandstand. Finnegan had loosened his firm grip on Proctor Knott, and the pride of Kentucky and Tennessee darted away from the Montana champion. In a few mighty strides, Proctor Knott led by three good lengths. The mile was completed in 1:45 1/4.

Spokane made a game effort, and Finnegan was inclined to use his whip urging Proctor Knott and taking no chances. The son of Luke Blackburn responded promptly and galloped easily home, the winner by two open lengths. Spokane finished second fighting off a hard drive by Retrieve, third. Once Again finished a poor fourth and was followed by Heron, Beth Broeck, and Glockner in that order.

Proctor Knott's finish in the mile and a quarter run was 2:12 1/4 and many, including Bryant, felt it could easily have been faster. In the mutuels, Proctor Knott paid $17.40 to win and $8 to place. Spokane paid $7.50 to place.

Joe Ullman and John F. Donovan, St. Louis bookmakers, won $5,000 each on Proctor Knott's success. Following the race, Ullman gave $100 to purchase an elegant blanket for the Kentucky winner. Perhaps this was an attempt to match the noble Knott's attire to the kingly robe of Spokane.

At last, Proctor Knott vanquished his Western rival. Sam Bryant commented, "He (Knott) was all right today, he has been feeding well and working nicely and putting up flesh, and he was able to run such a race as nobody around here has ever seen. I tell you when this hoss is right no hoss that ever eat oats could beat him a mile and a quarter, or a mile and a half. I expected to beat the record today, and if the track had been fast would have done it just as sure as the sun shines. I am going to ship him tomorrow night to Monmouth Park to run in the Lorillard Stakes the 9th of July. I wish it was four or five days further away than it is, because he will hit all the good ones they have got in the East, and I would like to have him just right so as to show these people what he can do. I don't like this thing shipping on there to run in a few days."

Bryant, feeling the winner again, finally accepted the blame for Knott's previous losses, saying it was all his fault. It had been wrong to take the big gelding to Nashville to run for $2,000 instead of keeping him home and taking care of him. Gone were the stories of poor riding and a drugged horse. Bryant needed no excuses for the Sheridan Stakes.

On the other side, Spokane lost. Explanations were demanded. Many believed the extra weight that the three-time victor, Spokane, carried was the cause of his defeat. Some said the distance, 1 1/4 mile, was not as suited for Spokane's style as was the longer 1 1/2 mile race. Others blamed the poor condition of the track. But believers of legend knew the cause. Spokane had won three major races in one season; two of these were Derbies, a feat never before accomplished. An Indian chief's prayer had been answered. That answer, a spirit horse to redeem the losses of his people, brought peace. With that peace came rest, and once at rest, the winning spirit departed Spokane.

At least one Kentuckian still held Spokane in high regard, Matt Winn, later President of Churchill Downs. He remembered the great racer fondly in this account taken from an article entitled "History of Racing in Washington" by Clio D. Hogan and printed in *The Washington Horse*:

"In 1888, Proctor Knott, a Kentucky-bred horse, won the running of the Belmont Futurity for two-year-olds. He was the sensational Thoroughbred of the season, and he came up to the Kentucky Derby of 1889 as the almost prohibitive betting favorite.

"The day before the race, I shuttled in and out of the barns doing like most youngsters do — sizing up the horses and trying to find some racer with a chance to beat the favorite. I had reached the stall which was occupied by Spokane, who was owned by the Montana Stable (Noah Armstrong) and had been shipped in from the West. Not much was known about him. But a little old fellow I knew as Bodie, a trainer, saw me looking at Spokane, and he said: 'Youngster, you're looking right now at the Derby winner tomorrow.'

"I was skeptical. But Bodie insisted Spokane couldn't lose. He finally convinced me and on Derby Day I took $110 off a none-too-thick bankroll and bet $100 for myself and $10 for Mrs. Winn on Spokane at 10 to 1. Spokane won by a nose, and I was $1,000 to the good.

"Mrs. Winn won $100 and her elation - it was only natural I guess because that was the first bet she had ever had on a horse - exceeded mine. But her brother was not too joyous. He had plunged on Proctor Knott.

"About a week later they met again - Proctor Knott and Spokane. That was in the Clark Handicap. Proctor Knott again was the favorite. Spokane was 4 to 1. I doubled my bet, getting $200 on Spokane, and Spokane came home in front, with my brother-in-law again backing the losing Proctor Knott.

"They moved on to Chicago to meet in the American Derby. For the third time, Proctor Knott was the favorite. Being in funds, I bet $400 on Spokane, and the odds were around 2 to 1. My brother-in-law backed Proctor Knott, but Spokane won his third straight.

"The Sheridan Handicap, also at Washington Park, Chicago, followed. That was about a week later. Both horses were entered. They finally made Spokane the favorite, and Proctor Knott was something like 3 to 1. I bet $500 of my $2,600 winnings - but this time, I was on Proctor Knott - not Spokane. My brother-in-law, finally having soured on Proctor Knott, also reversed himself. He bet on Spokane.

"Well, sir, that was the race in which Proctor Knott finally whipped Spokane, much to my youthful delight. And so, Spokane proved to be a right good friend of mine; winning for me when I backed him; losing when I was aboard his rival.

"The Spokane-Proctor Knott duels netted me a profit of about $4100 - a very large fortune back in the days of 1889."

On Tuesday, July 9, Spokane faced the Washington Park starter for a third time. The occasion was the Drexel Stakes, a one mile race with a value to the winner of $3,320. On a fine day and on a fast track, Spokane, in the company of six others, ran for victory.

In the odds, Spokane was entered at 5 to 2 as was Joe Courtney. Courtney carried 118 pounds compared to Spokane's 125. The California colt was ridden by Winchell while Kiley maintained control of Spokane. Champagne Charley, 118 pounds and ridden by jockey Eilke, was 8 to 1, and Come-to-Taw was 10 to 1. Come-to-Taw was under Blaylock and carried 120 pounds to the post. Heron, ridden by Lewis and bearing 118 pounds, was 15 to 1. The longest odds, 30 to 1, were shared by Vengeur, 118 pounds, jockey Seaman; and Angie Blackburn, 106 pounds, jockey Taral.

Champagne Charley broke in front, lapped by Vengeur, second, and Courtney, third. One length behind the leaders were Come-to-Taw and Angie Blackburn. Courtney followed them. In sixth position was Spokane. Heron trailed. Vengeur and Charley held the lead through the upper turn as they thundered toward home. Spokane, for a moment appearing his old self, advanced to third place one length behind the leaders. Kiley drove him hard, but the weight and pace dragged him down. Joe Courtney was sixth and considered beaten. One hundred yards from the finish Champagne Charley and Vengeur fought for first. Vengeur yielded, and Come-to-Taw advanced. It appeared that one of these two, Champagne Charley or Come-to-Taw would win. Suddenly, a shout rattled the stands as Courtney came flying from the rear.

"Courtney! Courtney wins! See him come!"

Whipped to action and spurred for speed, Champagne Charley drew away from Come-to-Taw, Vengeur, and Spokane, but he could not overcome the irresistible rush of Courtney. Safely in front, Winchell eased the Californian up, creating a dangerous finish only a neck in front of Champagne Charley. Come-to-Taw, two lengths behind, was third; followed by Vengeur, fourth; Spokane, fifth; Heron, a poor sixth; and Annie Blackburn, seventh and last.

Spokane was again beaten, and a fickle public quickly courted new victors. But in Montana, the name Spokane still evoked reverent devotion and ecstatic emotion.

In Great Falls on July 14, 1889, the President of Montana's Constitutional Convention and Butte's great copper king, the Honorable William A. Clark, spoke to businessmen about the prospects of the soon-to-be state's promising future: "...I might speak of other things in which Montana excels. I might refer to the fact that we have the most beautiful women that can be found anywhere. I might mention another fact, that next to a beautiful woman, in the estimation of all well-educated gentlemen, a fine horse is next in order and haven't we got Spokane? Spokane, the prince of the turf, who beat the great blood of the Blue Grass region of Kentucky. Gentlemen, we are going to have a great state here..."

Mr. Clark's remarks were met with loud applause.

Although Spokane was next scheduled to run July 24 at St. Paul, Minnesota, in the Twin City Derby, he was scratched. William B. Hundley, Noah Armstrong's partner in the Montana Stable made this statement to the *Helena Independent*:

"When we entered Spokane in the Twin City Derby, we were determined to start in any event and could have done so had he been in proper condition. He is not. The trouble is he has had too much work and is not in condition. He is in fact in the hands of the veterinarian and has been for the past three weeks. No horse in the country has done the work Spokane has. He has won three of the greatest stakes in the country: the Kentucky Derby, the Clark Stakes, and the American Derby. Each win added to his penalty. It was this extra weight and the heavy track on which he ran recently that threw the horse off. It is our intention now to ship him to Saratoga. The very best place in the world for horses to recuperate their strength. Mr. Armstrong was willing and would have permitted Spokane to have been exhibited here, but myself and my trainer objected to this. We both recognized what a disappointment his nonappearance would be to the people of the Northwest, but we would not risk the long ride as he was not fitted for the race. I insisted on his not doing anymore travel and if he can get into condition, he will finish his engagements in the East. If not, we will rest him as long as necessary. By our not coming to Helena (Montana), we are out fully $500 in forfeits, etc. No blame can rest upon the management for the nonappearance of our stable. Secretary Sherman offered us every inducement, but it could not be done. No one regrets the termination affairs have taken more than Mr. Armstrong and myself."

The Westchester Stakes were listed as next on Spokane's schedule. This was to be held on August 20, 1889. Spokane did not run. Despite his recent misfortunes, Spokane was not for sale. He was the first great race horse Montana had ever produced, and emphatically his owner declared, he would continue a Montana property.

Spokane did sufficiently recover in time to race twice more in 1889. In New York on August 31, 1889, Armstrong entered Spokane in the 1 1/4 mile Pelham Bay Handicap for three-year-olds. Facing odds of 5 to 1, Spokane met Tenny, another 125 pound candidate at odds of 2 to 1. Spokane, under a new rider, Garrison, placed third in this encounter. Tenny, ridden by Hamilton, was the clear winner by three lengths. He romped home in a canter.

On September 3, 1889 at Coney Island (Sheepshead Bay), New York, in the 1 1/4 mile Twin City Handicap, the public's declining faith in any of the three-year-old favorites was revealed. Retrieve, Proctor Knott, and Spokane were all at odds of 10 to 1. A large field of twelve horses competed for the $4,725 prize. Spokane finished in seventh place. Proctor Knott was fifth and Retrieve, sixth. Spokane's weight was a mere 112 pounds, but even this welcome release was not enough. Exile, carrying 125 pounds, was the winner.

From fire to flickering flame, the cost of Spokane's previous victories was high. Like the snow that vanishes in the wake of a Montana chinook, so was the bright glory of Spokane, generous gift and fleeting light from the spirit world. □

19 Glory Enough

Montana became the forty-first state of the United States of America on November 8, 1889, only six months after Spokane's Kentucky Derby triumph. Between 1880 and 1890, the population of Montana officially grew from 39,000 to 143,000. New York author L. E. Quigg said of Montana, "The chief evil of this Northwestern country is the tendency of everybody to work himself to death. You must keep going as the crowd goes. You can't lag behind while those around you are hurling themselves forward."

"Hurling" they were. This same author commented on Butte, Montana, saying, "One does as much living in ten years in Butte as he can do in twenty in the East." In Helena, citizens boasted of their city's railway, commercial, and political centrality, citing these as valid reasons for making Helena the permanent capital of the new state.

Great growth was predicted for Montana in view of her "natural advantages, and her pushing, forceful people." Montana was touted as "one of the most beautiful regions on the globe." Her "natural advantages" included three major industries: agriculture, mining, and lumber. Her climate was considered amiable, being "regulated throughout the summer months by cool, invigorating breezes from her snow-capped mountains." Blessed by abundant water for irrigation, Montana mountains served as a great reservoir. Clear, fresh, and flowing streams meant ample water power. Thus, the opportunity for manufacturing existed on a grand scale.

Silent, lofty peaks held buried treasure beneath mounds of earth and snow. Mineral wealth flourished. There were great quantities of silver, gold, lead, copper, coal, and iron to be mined. Prospecting was considered in its infancy; Montana was yet a frontier.

Cattle, sheep, and horses were profitably raised. Montana valleys yielded fine crops. Immense forests of deciduous and evergreen trees hid within their perimeters indigenous supplies of huckleberries, raspberries, gooseberries, plums, currants, and wild cherries.

The open ranges of Montana, Wyoming, Idaho, Washington, and Oregon produced annually thousands of horses in excess of their needs. Grown to maturity on nutritious bunch grass, these animals developed tremendous lung power from the thin, clear air as they scampered wildly over the prairies. The dry soil was said to encourage the growth of hard, symmetrical hooves, and the native forage was thought to produce remarkable muscles. Improved by the introduction of Kentucky Thoroughbreds into the area, locally bred animals rose to a level of high quality. Miles City, Montana, established a market for this fine stock and hoped to eventually gain a national reputation equal to that of Lexington, Kentucky.

Montana's area, 147,138 square miles, far exceeded the demands of her relatively few residents. People from the East were encouraged to "take note of these facts." The local populace, meanwhile, was urged to consider the condition of others and see that they had little cause for complaint. *The Northwest Magazine* of February 1890 concluded its Montana account by cautioning citizens to, "Look around you, make the best of what you have, and feel contented."

Marcus Daly of Anaconda, a wealthy copper magnate, developed a great horse ranch near present-day Hamilton, Montana. Calling the area, Riverside, it was a young town in March of 1890. The animals residing there represented a quarter of a million dollars in investment. They included Mascot, Favonia, Yolo Maid, St. Valor, "Mike," Hattie D., Lord Byron, Prodigal, Senator, St. Patrick, Brown Silk, Fannie Witherspoon, and Boston. They were all either racing or trotting horses.

In Helena for a visit, Noah Armstrong talked with reporters on March 17, 1890. He was enroute from his Seattle residence to Kentucky to oversee the readying of his Montana Stable for the 1890 season. The *Helena Independent* announced:

"Mr. Armstrong has great hopes of Spokane's success in the Surburban Handicap. He says that the great Derby winner will be in better trim than he was for the Kentucky Derby. Then he was trained down too fine, and after he had won the American Derby at Chicago, he was as thin as he should have been in September after a season's racing. He says horses never ran a worse track than Washington Park the day the Derby was run. It was very muddy after a two weeks rain, and he says Proctor Knott's jockey did a wise thing in pulling up the colt after the mile was run. That was what saved him for the rest of the season. Spokane was knocked out there. Don Jose fared even worse, and Sorrento was rendered useless."

Mr. Armstrong spoke well of Kiley and mentioned that he would be Spokane's rider in the Surburban.

Of Spokane's style, Mr. Armstrong related, ". . . the colt is a great loafer. He leads his trainer to believe he is doing his best when he is only playing."

In addition to Spokane, the Montana Stable had twelve other hopeful racers in 1890. One, Umatilla, a full sister of Spokane's, was expected to do very well and was entered in the Futurity. A new trainer was added, L. Elmore, and Armstrong held high expectations, holding that "the Montana Stable will at least win its feed bill."

Reports on March 28, 1890, indicated that Noah Armstrong had brought two carloads of fine colts from his Twin Bridges farm to be shipped to Louisville by way of the Northern Pacific Railway. The colts were stabled at the old Breck and Fisher Stable in Helena.

Noah proudly displayed the youngsters to visitors. They included Silver Star, a half sister of Spokane by Tom Bowling. Silver Star was described as a gray roan yearling, tall for her age, with finely-shaped limbs and every inch a race horse. She was entered for the $100,000 Futurity Stake to be run in 1891. Another promising-looking yearling stood near Silver Star. Broad of limb and thin, this one was considered by the Helena reporter to be a better animal than the Futurity candidate. His dam was by Wheeler T., a record breaker of high quality.

In an area adjoining this stable, stood a two-year-old bay horse named Lavina by Hyder Ali; second dam an Arabian mare by King Richard. Patting Lavina's splendid broad back, Noah bragged, "That colt isn't far from the Arabian desert." Lacking six weeks of being a full two-years-old, Lavina's flesh was hard, his limbs well developed, and he was reputed to be a fast runner in the pasture.

Next was Eveline, another two-year-old by Hyder Ali. Completing the show were two prospective brood mares. One a full sister to Spokane was to be bred to Glen Elm. The second, a filly by Tom Bowling out of Hermine by Alarm, was picked by Armstrong to be bred to Spokane. At this time, Mr. Armstrong boasted a total of twenty Thoroughbred brood mares under his ownership. Accompanying these quality representatives of the racing world was Noah's treasured supply of Montana hay and oats. His racers deserved the finest in feed.

Also on March 28, of that year, the *Spokane Review* reported on the condition of Proctor Knott. They related how he had wintered well and described him as fat and hardy. Allowed to run wild on the Scoggan farm, he was at least 400 pounds heavier than when he started for the American Derby. Bryant's routine was universally blamed for his disappointing three-year-old season, and a different system was proposed. His trainer, S. Wheeler, planned on taking Knott first to Nashville. Wheeler believed he would lose that, his first race of the season. From there, Proctor Knott was to go to Louisville, Latonia, and then east to prepare for the Surburban. The Surburban was expected to be the only Eastern spring event in which Knott would start. From thence, he would travel west for the Chicago Wheeler Handicap and other events at Washington Park.

Of Spokane it was disclosed: "(He) has wintered finely and is fat and has grown. His weak leg is all right and his health is perfect. He has not yet been galloped. His trainer thinks he will hardly be ready until a Louisville meeting, when he will meet Proctor Knott and the pick of the Kentucky stables in the Merchant's Handicap. From there, he goes to Latonia and Chicago and possibly east."

Colonel William B. Hundley, Noah Armstrong's partner who owned a one-half interest in the Montana Stables, sold out his interest to Mr. Armstrong, it was revealed on April 2, 1890. Noah was now the sole owner of such racers as Rimini, a bay mare; Meckie H., a chestnut mare; Polemus, a bay colt; and Dafrus, a bay colt. No purchase price was reported. All the horses, with the exception of Dafrus, were in Louisville along with Spokane, Tacoma, Craw Fish, and Orcas.

A correspondent for the *Chicago Horseman* visited Churchill Downs and wrote: "The Montana Stable was the next place visited. Its champion is Spokane. L. Elmore received me cordially and needed but little encouragement to be induced to talk of Spokane, although he is not of a loquacious disposition. 'This is last year's Derby winner,' he said, with pardonable pride as he opened the stall door. There, up to his knees in fresh straw, stood the famous son of Hyder Ali. He stuck his blazed face out of the door as soon as it was opened and affectionately shoved his nose into his trainer's bosom. Intelligence beamed from his bright eyes, and every hair on his sleek sides gave token of health and strength.

"How is he getting on? I asked. 'Couldn't be better,' was the trainer's sententious reply. We entered the stall and looked the handsome chestnut over from tip to toe, and if there is a blemish on him it was not revealed to two eager pair of eyes. His legs are clean and his well-developed chest and rounded barrel show that he has filled out considerably. 'That was a great race last Derby day, wasn't it?' said Mr. Elmore, with a suspicion of a sigh. I heartily agreed with him. 'Not likely to occur again soon,' he continued, and I subscribed to this proposition as heartily as I had to the previous one. Then conversation turned to Proctor Knott, who is now being carefully trained at his owner's stables across the country from Churchill Downs... Both horses are in good form.''

When asked about the Derby candidates for 1890, Mr. Elmore replied, "I don't think much of any of them so far, and I don't look for much of a race; nothing to compare with last year." He was right. A horse named Riley, ridden by Isaac Murphy, won by one and three-quarter lengths. It wasn't close.

Proctor Knott reached the 1890 season sound, it seemed, though there was evidence that he had struck one of his forelegs while romping in his paddock over the winter. It was a little sore and painful, but his trainer blistered and bandaged it. Now the red flannel wrap was gone, and Proctor Knott appeared flawless. Sam Bryant was happy.

"Spokane moved for the first time this spring out of an ordinary gallop," it was noted by the *Helena Independent* of April 20, 1890. "He seems to favor his game leg considerably and is quite likely to go down in the other leg in trying to save the one that is already lame."

In the opinion of this author, Spokane's most important 1890 race would be against his old antagonist, Proctor Knott. The battle, he felt, would test which one got tired first, and he did not believe either capable of winning any great events this season. The notion of the writer was that though Armstrong had quite a large stable in training, none of them possessed a promising outlook.

By May 25, Spokane's once bright future grew dimmer. The *Helena Independent* disclosed:

"The discouraging news has been announced that Spokane, Montana's pride and winner of the fastest Kentucky Derby on record, is laid up with pleura-pneumonia. While this has not been verified by Mr. Armstrong, the fact that the great son of Hyder Ali is being declared out of the big eastern events gives the report every color of truth, but Montanians earnestly hope that the horse may come around all right and be heard from before the season is over."

From Louisville, reports on June 1st indicated little progress on Spokane's health. Though the great flyer appeared well bodily, his astute managers only shook their heads when asked about his prospects for that year. The disease that afflicted Spokane did its work, and only Old Father time could tell when the Montana favorite again would face the starter.

New York accounts were equally disheartening, ". . . last year's Derby winner, Spokane is slowly recovering from his supposed attack of lung fever and is now pronounced out of danger by the veterinary attending him. That authority states that the attack will prevent him from being prepared for racing this year."

Yet despite these persistent rumors, Spokane went to the post on June 7th for the Latonia Sweepstakes, a race of one mile. This was a highly touted race, pitting Spokane and Proctor Knott against each other once more. Neither of them even placed. The event was won by Newcastle, a clear length in front. Carrying 115 pounds and ridden by R. Williams, Spokane finished fourth amongst the field of seven. His arch rival, Proctor Knott, at the same weight, finished fifth. Spokane lost the race, but he did have the satisfaction of vanquishing Proctor Knott one final time, making the record of their matches, Spokane, 4; Proctor Knott, 2.

Encouraged, Noah entered Spokane in a $600 Purse race at Chicago's

Washington Park on Monday, June 23. Winning the fourth race of 1 1/16 mile with the horse Craw Fish, Armstrong felt very lucky as Spokane took the track for the fifth and final race of the day, a 1 1/8 mile run. Only four horses were entered. Spokane bore 108 pounds and was ridden by Pike Barnes, ironically the pilot who had guided Proctor Knott in the famed Kentucky Derby. The betting favorite at 5 to 3 odds, Spokane made a fine stretch run, and placed second, beaten only a head by T. H. Steven's entry, Wary.

Eager to win, Noah waited only three days before running Spokane in another Purse race at Washington Park. The distance was 1 1/4 mile, and the date was Thursday, June 26. A small field of five awaited the tap of the starter's drum. The Montana colt was second in the odds at 7 to 5. Carrying 113 pounds, Spokane was again guided by Pike Barnes. Waiting his usual game, Spokane rushed in the straight at the finish, but failed to reach the winner, Robespierre. The latter won by a nose. Spokane pulled up slightly lame.

For the Montana Stable, the good fortune that blessed its 1889 season, vanished in 1890. Dr. Long, a veterinary surgeon, returned to Helena after visiting the Doncaster Farm of Noah Armstrong. He had been called to attend the mare, Interpose, dam of Spokane. She had been injured in the pasture. The grass was wet, and she twisted her leg while rising from the ground. The leg broke. Dr. Long built a sling for Interpose and tried to save her. Interpose was valued at $10,000 and produced four fast horses. She had a suckling colt at her side by Tom Bowling. Many felt he was not proven as a sire and believed Armstrong would have been wiser to have bred Interpose to Hyder Ali, now the possession of Marcus Daly and residing at his Montana Bitter Root Farm. It was felt that this union would enhance the possibility of acquiring another quality Thoroughbred like Spokane. The argument was now academic.

Of Spokane himself, the distinguished Montana horseman, Mr. B. C. Kingsbury of Butte, said, "He is always a splendid animal to look upon, but this time he gave me the impression of being stale and over-worked. His color was dull and the hair did not have that bright glossy appearance which shows good physical condition and perfect training. To me, he had the appearance of having been run to death, and that I fancy is about what his trainer did with him last season. That he is thoroughly out of condition is shown by the fact that he was beaten by Wary."

Spokane went to the post one last time on July 2, 1890. It was again at Washington Park in Chicago. His rider was Monahan. The field was small, only four horses. Spokane carried 112 pounds. The distance was the longest of his career, two miles. Outbound won by a length over Hypocrite, second. The weary Spokane finished third, a half a length behind Hypocrite. Hamlet was last.

Twin City Derby ribbon. Armstrong family collection.

Though Spokane was not winning, large Montana horse farms made the national news almost daily. These included: Marcus Daly's Bitter Root Farm, S. E. Larabees', Huntley and Clarke's, Raymond Bros.' Belmont Park Farms, Hugh Kirkendall's, and of course, Noah Armstrong's Montana Stable. Ben Kingsbury, a colt bred by Kohr and Bielenberg of Deer Lodge and owned by B. C. Kingsbury, placed second in the American Derby.

On July 30, Noah's luck changed for the better. In the Minneapolis Stakes at the Twin City meet, his two-year-old colt, Ranier, broke a world's record for the five and one half furlongs at his age classification. His time was 1:08 1/4. Ranier prevailed over a field of fifteen. He faced odds of 15 to 1 in this, his first major performance. At Latonia on October 18, Armstrong's Rimini won the mile race on that meet's closing day.

Ten Montana horses belonging to Noah Armstrong and H. R. Baker were on the Eastern circuit in 1890. This small band picked off large and small chunks of the stakes and purses. They proved themselves breadwinners of no little merit. Nevada, Meckie H., Warpeak, Argenta, Rimini, and Daniel B. showed their dust to many of the season's noted flyers.

Montana trotting horses were making news as well. Florida trotted away from a field of three-year-olds in Colorado, earning the fast time of 2:26 1/4. Trainers even sent horses to "vacation" in Montana's bracing climate to build their lung capacity. The California trotter, Homestake, was here for seven months, and when returned to harness racing, he surprised everyone with his grace, speed, and endurance.

The *Northwest Magazine,* quoting from the *White Sulphur Springs Husbandman,* scoffed at those who would christen Montana the Bonanza State, saying that it was long before titled the Bunch Grass State. This nickname was earned on "a hotly-contested field" through the merits of a plant that many believed imparted elastic muscles and toughened sinews to the Montana horse. Bunch grass also was acknowledged to contribute to great tasting beef and mutton. Though Colorado and Nevada also grew bunch grass, Montana's product was the first to bring its merits to the fore.

By 1890, Montana's business of breeding and raising horses attained such a degree of prominence that it was placed among the important industries of the state. Following the example set by Noah Armstrong and Spokane, Marcus Daly and other Montana millionaires drifted into the business. In November of 1890, it was reported that Daly had purchased over $160,000 worth of horses "bred in the purple." Brought from Europe to Montana, there were less than thirteen steeds in the group. Of these, three were priced at $80,000. They represented the finest brood mares and stallions available at the time. Daly did not restrict his purchases to the state of Kentucky or even the North American continent.

While Montana breeders sought to bring the best into their state, others felt that they already produced the best. Headlines proclaimed, "Blue Grass and Bunch Grass States Swapping Horses."

Returning to Helena from Cincinnati on November 12, 1890, Mr. Armstrong was the subject of an interview. The *Helena Independent* reported: "Noah Armstrong is looking hale and hearty, but was a good deal like Rip Van Winkle concerning matters at home. He had not heard that Interpose, the dam of Spokane had broken her leg, nor did he know that his farm produced the best two and three-year-old trotting filly in the Northwest." That horse was Florida, and she was the property of Dr. Long, the Armstrong veterinarian, ample payment for his valuable services.

Confirming reports of Spokane's retirement, Noah stated that the king was now at the Woolley Breeding Farm near Lexington, Kentucky, where a number of brood mares would be mated to him in the spring. Armstrong predicted that the great horse probably would never be brought to Montana again.

Of his miserable luck, Armstrong stated that every one of his fourteen head were sick with pneumonia at different times, but in succession. He frequently was compelled to "scratch" them only the day before they were to race. He disclosed the sale of Meckie H. and Rimini by saying that they could not pack the weight. Rimini, it was revealed, had ringbone in one leg. This caused it to swell out whenever she started on a hot day over a dry track.

Pinning his 1891 hopes on Wallula, a colt by Tom Bowling, and Ranier by Bazarro, Noah Armstrong paused to fondly recall the 1889 Kentucky Derby:

"I don't believe we will live to see another race like that one, nor shall we see such fast time recorded at such an early season by young horses. I believe that was the greatest field of three-year-olds ever got together for a race. That it was a race is best shown from the fact that since it was run about all the starters have broken down. The horses were too evenly matched, and that made the struggle the greater. It was too early in the year for such a strain on three-year-olds. Once Again, one of the finest animals I ever saw has never been fit for anything since. His first defeat broke his heart. Come-to-Taw and Hindoocraft and Proctor Knott, and Spokane, too, were of little account after that memorable struggle. But I expect to see Proctor come out on the track next year in good shape. Spokane is all right where he is. He was broken down in his stall. The trainer did something for which I released him, but that was poor satisfaction for the loss of Spokane's engagements which he could not fill in consequence."

After spending a few days at his Montana ranch, Noah was expected to winter in Seattle, caring for his business interests there.

Despite his personal setbacks, Armstrong's accomplishments benefited Montana horse breeders for years to come. Even the famed James B. Haggin was "of Montana" in 1892. The *Helena Independent* described this phenomenon:

"Spokane was the first example that opened the eyes of turfdom, and though he retires to the stud, he leaves the turf with glory enough for a lifetime." □

20 Spirituelle

A kaleidoscope of change occurred in the era of the 1890's. Horseless carriages were in the early stages of their development, the concept of their practicality gaining in both strength and popularity. The phonograph was in use. One determined young couple even employed this new medium in the instrumentation of their marriage.

In February of 1891, it was already very evident that Proctor Knott was once again an object of much speculation. The Scoggan's Brothers were accused of scaring Knott's would-be detractors by spinning outlandish yarns about the big gelding's remarkable private workouts. From Louisville came reports that Proctor Knott was fully recovered from the lameness that attacked him so inopportunely the previous spring. Doctored at Sheepshead Bay, New York, during the summer of 1890, the results were described as 'glorious.' Mr. Scoggan firmly stated that Proctor was as sound as he had ever been in his life. Predicted a big money winner for 1891, Proctor Knott had been working all winter. Knott was scheduled to arrive in Memphis at the beginning of March to begin preparations for the upcoming season. His program was an ambitious one. The great son of Luke Blackburn was entered in the following stakes: the Manhattan Handicap and Country Club in New York; the Delbach Handicap in Louisville; the Straus Handicap in Lexington; the Merchant's and Decoration Handicap at Latonia; and the Wheeler Handicap, Oakwood Handicap, and Boulevard Handicap in Chicago at Washington Park.

It was not thoughts of race tracks, horses, and high stakes that drove Noah Armstrong forward in the spring of 1891; it was gold, Alaska gold. On the skirts of Yaketa Bay along the Alaskan coast, a small island beckoned. It possessed a base of solid rock, and its sandy covering was thoroughly impregnated with fine gold in significant quantities. Discovered by Armstrong and his friend and partner, John A. Van Brocklin, in 1886, work on the claim was delayed as other enterprises took precedence. But in 1891, circumstances allowed the mining to begin, and Mr. Armstrong was confident its yield would equal, if not surpass, that of Alder Gulch in Virginia City, Montana.

Noah Armstrong's glory days on the eastern tracks ended with the career of Spokane, but July of 1891 still found him a central figure at Washington Park. *The Chicago Herald* reported that Armstrong was so successful in placing his bets that he had to avoid being followed. When he laid $100 on a horse, word spread, and the odds changed. To avert such happenings, Armstrong usually sent his money into the ring by special messenger. When pressed to answer the ever-present question, "What do you like, Mr. Armstrong?", his reply was invariably, "Whiskey and sugar."

This article stated, "There are many things that Mr. Armstrong would have taken apart and readjusted if he had been superintending the earth. Few things make him as ruffled in temper as to have someone say, 'I've got it straight from the stable that this horse can't lose.'"

To that Mr. Armstrong was heard to reply, "These touts would ruin the temper of an angel and break a mint in less than a month. Half the time the owners and trainers don't know how good their horses are. I remember once when I was going to start Grey Cloud in a race a few years ago down at Latonia. I thought he had a good chance to win it, and made up my mind to back him. The morning of the race, I went out to see him gallop, and when he came in I asked my trainer what he thought of the chances, and he said: 'Mr. Armstrong, we're not in it. Grey Cloud won't be in the neighborhood at the finish.'"

Noah asked, "Then you wouldn't advise me to back him?"

"Well, I should say not. Don't you risk a lead dollar with a hole in it on his chances," came the quick and depressing response.

"This was not very encouraging," Noah continued, "but when they began selling auction pools that afternoon, I hung around the box, and as everybody in the crowd seemed to have a tip that my horse was no good there was no one but me to bid on him, so I bought him in every pool. People began joshing me about the long waves I would have to walk to get home, and I began to get a little warm and started down the line, giving the bookmakers a little argument about Grey Cloud at long odds. By the time the race started, I had enough Grey Cloud tickets in my breast pocket to make it bulge out as if I was carrying a small loaf of bread for lunch.

"It was only a big gallop for Grey Cloud, and he won by several lengths. When the race was over the trainer rushed up to me and said, 'Did you back him, Mr. Armstrong?'"

Mr. Armstrong replied cleverly, "Just a few dollars, a little loose change that I had in my pocket."

"My God!" the trainer exclaimed with a groan. "I don't see why you didn't make a plunge on him. I thought it was the surest thing that I ever saw in my life."

Noah then concluded his story, "The liar can never be a success unless he has a good memory, and these race track touts talk so much and tell so many different stories to different men that very few of them can remember just what they have said, and so are in constant danger of being caught in the Annanias act."

Misfortune struck at Washington Park in 1891. The Montana horse, High Tariff, in Chicago for the American Derby, fell dead on the track. Bred in Deer Lodge, the Eastin and Larabee colt was the winner of the Clark Stakes and Latonia Derby.

On August 6, 1891, the well-known race horse, Proctor Knott, died in his stall at Horsehaven in Saratoga, New York. He never achieved the degree of health that the Scoggans described in the spring.

Proctor Knott was eulogized for his famed two-year-old twin victories in the Junior Champion and Futurity Stakes of 1888. Sam Bryant and his partner, George W. Scoggan, had paid only $425 for the noble chestnut as a yearling, and the superior gelding returned them more than $100,000 over the three short seasons of his career.

The reason for Spokane's sudden disappearance from the track was now public. Alluded to by Noah Armstrong in his interview of November 12, 1890, "The trainer did something for which I released him," the *Seattle Press-Times* of Tuesday, October 15, 1891, reported:

"Spokane, like all race horses of delicate organization was very nervous and one day when he was sleeping soundly in his stall a boy, wishing to awaken him for some purpose, struck him with a pitchfork. The horse started to his feet suddenly and broke one of the tendons in his foreleg. From this he recovered so as to show no lameness, but his usefulness as a race horse was forever past, as it has been proven that the tendon would give way if strained in a race."

This unhappy incident occurred, the account states, during the winter of 1889, before Spokane's 1890 races. Mindful of this, the courage of Spokane was remarkable. As a four-year-old, he had run four races, earned one fifth, one third, and two seconds. The seconds were near misses, one lost by a head, the other by a nose. All of this was accomplished following his severe leg injury.

A chestnut stallion, his coat like burnished gold, lounged about the Fairhaven Stock Farm, five miles from Lexington, Kentucky, on the Parker's Mill Pike. The proprietor of the farm, Robert W. Woolley, Jr., advertised that for a fifty dollar fee, worthy mares could be serviced by this famed racer, Spokane.

The historic duels of Spokane and Proctor Knott were forever ended, but the competition between Montana and Kentucky Thoroughbreds persisted.

Marcus Daly purchased the famed Tammany in 1890 for $2,500. By August of 1891, Tammany already was a winner, having collected the $24,500 first prize in the Great Eclipse Stakes, an important two-year-old event. The racer, Montana, added $17,000 in winnings to the account. Sir Matthew, claimed victory in the Junior Champion Stakes, and another $24,000 lined the coffers of the copper king.

A flamboyant figure, Marcus Daly once spent two million dollars to gain election to office. He lost. At one point in 1891, he had 219 personal entries on a single track, Monmouth Park. In betting his horses, he was notorious. Once he had a $40,000 ticket in a shirt pocket. The ticket was on Tammany, one of his favorites. Tammany won the race. Daly's shirt went to the laundry, the valuable ticket still in the pocket.

Marcus Daly continued to be a major factor in the turf world until his death on November 12, 1900. It was said that he suffered from dilation of the heart and Bright's disease of the kidneys. Daly was only fifty-eight at the time of his death, but he had accomplished a great deal in that short time. Horses were his chief source of pleasure, and conservative estimates were that he expended more than a million dollars on blooded stock. He owned Hamburg, purchased by him for $40,000 when the colt was but a two-year-old. Hamburg proved a champion both on the track and as a sire. Tammany won such famous races as the Surburban, the Great Eclipse Stakes, the Withers, the Jerome Handicap, and the Lorillard. He so endeared himself to his owner that his image was inlaid onto the wooden lobby floor of Marcus Daly's Montana Hotel in Anaconda, Montana.

Well-known stakes were taken by Daly's steeds. A colt named Montana won the Suburban. Ogden won the prestigious Futurity, and Scottish Chieftain claimed the Belmont Stakes of 1897.

Daly retired from the eastern racing circuit in 1897, citing the pressures of business, "I cannot continue the hope of seeing my horses work and run. There is not much sport in reading about the doings of one's own horses. If I could watch them in their preparations and then see them struggle to win, I should feel less dissatisfied. A racing stable in the east is expensive...The racing in Montana is a very jolly affair. The circuit lasts sixty days. I shall keep a small stable to compete in these events...I shall continue my breeding farm in Montana."

So saying, Daly shipped four carloads of his string home on September 16 under the able care of his trainer, Matt Byrnes.

The dispersal of the Daly estate included the sale of eight stallions, 104 brood mares, and 75 horses in training. Held at Madison Square Garden, New York, on January 30, 31, and February 1, 1901, it was conducted by the Fasig-Tipton Company. Mr. Edward Tipton was the

> **MAXWELTON STOCK FARM.**
>
> —o—
>
> # SPOKANE,
>
> (Winner of the Maiden Two-Year-Old Stake, at Latonia; also winner of the Kentucky Derby, Clark Stakes, and American Derby).
>
> Sire of J. Walter, Rheinstrom, Spokena, Sir Loin, Amy T., Three Forks, and Mehama.
>
> Chestnut horse, 16 hands high, foaled 1886, by Hyder Ali; 1st dam Interpose, by Imp. Intruder; 2d dam Lilac, by Lightning; 3d dam Dolly Carter, by imp. Glencoe; &c., will make the season of 1897 at Maxwelton Stock Farm, four miles from Lexington on the Winchester pike, at
>
> **PRIVATE CONTRACT.**
>
> For further information address or call on
>
> 1146Jy1   B. T. HUME, Box 248, Lexington, Ky.

Advertisement for Spokane at stud, Maxwelton Stock Farm. Appeared in the Thoroughbred Record *of September, 1897. This is the last official record of Spokane.*

Manager of the Daly Stable. The great Tammany graced the cover of the *Spirit of the Times* for January 5, 1901, in an advertisement for the impending sale.

Spokane continued in Kentucky living in luxurious retirement. He left the Fairhaven Stock Farm at the end of the 1892 season. Moving closer to Lexington, only three miles on the Winchester Pike, he was placed in the charge of James P. McCann of the Niddervale Stock Farm. His stud fee was still $50. Spokane remained there through the 1894 season.

In March of 1892, Fred T. Counter, the manager of Noah Armstrong's ranch at Twin Bridges, talked with a reporter from the *Dillon Tribune*. Mr. Counter had heartening news of Spokane, voicing that, "In all probability, he (Spokane) will be back on the track again in the course of a year or two." He also related the tale of Spokane's injury, but his version said that the shock of being so suddenly awakened caused Spokane to fall and wrench his spinal column. This comment contradicted the 1891 report of a torn tendon. In any case, the injury was so severe that many thought Spokane never would recover. In this interview, Mr. Counter reported Spokane's condition so improved that even the best veterinary surgeons had changed their minds and did not rule out Spokane's complete recovery.

Spokane's 1892 offspring were both fillies; one a chestnut, the other, a bay. Both dams were by Tom Bowling.

In 1893, Spokane sired three more: one bay filly, a brown colt, and a chestnut colt. The chestnut was christened Spokesman.

C. J. Enright next contracted the services of Spokane. Still owned by Noah Armstrong, Spokane was housed at the Elmendorf Stables, also of Lexington, through the seasons of 1895 and 1896.

Spokane's get was racing in 1895, garnering a total of $2,985 in prizes. The biggest money winner was Three Forks with $2,425. The sum total increased in 1896 to $5,897. Three Forks again topped the list of winners with $2,732 for his efforts. Amy T., Dew of June, J. Walter, Kennie Thatcher, Old Nassau, Rheinstrom, and Spokena also contributed.

The 1897 season found Spokane at the Maxwelton Stock Farm, still of Lexington. He was under the care of B.T. Hume. Here Spokane remained until approximately September 18. That is the date of his last advertisement for stud in *The Thoroughbred Record*.

From this point on, the history of Spokane becomes speculative. Marcus Daly shipped horses to Montana on September 16th of 1897. Perhaps Spokane hitched a ride.

Noah Armstrong sold out his interest in the Montana ranch to Max Lauterbach in 1900. Noah died in Seattle on April 21, 1907, after an illness of only two months. Mr. Armstrong had resided in Seattle on a permanent basis since 1901. At the time of his death, Mr. Armstrong was 84 years of age.

John Rodegap, Spokane's Louisville trainer of the famed 1889 season, died in May of 1913. He was a prominent and respected turf figure. Mr. Rodegap almost had the honor of training two Derby winners. Inventor, the second-place horse of the 1902 Kentucky Derby, lost by a nose. Official records chided, "The jockey on Inventor waited too long."

March of 1914 brought the death of Thomas Kiley, Spokane's valiant jockey. In his later years, Kiley had become a veteran trainer, campaigning his own stable over Western tracks.

As might be expected of a legend, various stories of the mighty Spokane emerged over the years. His death remains a mystery, though many attempts have been made to resolve it. Most published accounts subscribe to the belief that the great racer died shortly after his successful 1889 season, but irrefutable evidence shows that Spokane was a valued stud through mid-September of 1897.

Homer Faust for the *Tribune* of Shelby, on May 16, 1932, wrote: "Brought back to Montana, he (Spokane) was accorded the hero worship that was justly his. Horsemen from every corner of the state journeyed to Twin Bridges to do him honor, and mention of his name was alone sufficient to thrill the heart of proud Montanans. That he never again so distinguished himself was unimportant — he had won the Derby and broke the record. He had well earned the right to rest upon his laurels."

Royal Brougham of the *Seattle Post-Intelligencer* wrote on April 29, 1948: "The October 15, 1891 edition of the *Press-Times* briefly records the end of the horse —Spokane died from the injuries received when a farm hand tried to awaken him with a pitchfork. He broke one of his tendons...'"

When checked, records reveal this account in error on one major point. The quote is a misquote. Nowhere does the article cited say Spokane died, only that he was injured and "Lost to the Turf: Stallion Spokane Forever Ruined for the Track."

Another article, this by Grace Roffey Pratt writing for the *Western Horseman* in January of 1976, says: "With 17-year-old Jim Dempsey, a Montana lad, as rider, Spokane was running strong when he stumbled and fell. Young Dempsey was thrown and killed. It was Spokane's last race. Armstrong retired him to the ranch where he remained the rest of his life. Some believe he was injured in the fall and not able to race again. Others felt Armstrong was so saddened by the death of his young jockey that he had no heart to again race the horse that caused the fatal accident."

Parts of this story are true. There was a young Montana man named John Dempsey, not Jim, who rode races for Noah Armstrong. He was killed in Chicago at Garfield Park. However, there is no John Dempsey listed as Spokane's jockey of record for any of his starts.

Billy Dingley, another Montanan, was rumored to have ridden Spokane in the famed Kentucky Derby. Though there is little doubt that Dingley could have ridden the racer at some point in his life, this particular tale is not substantiated by any official records.

Ralph Bidwell for the *Great Falls Tribune* wrote on May 7, 1977, that following the Sheridan Stakes of 1889, Spokane was shipped home. "Along the way, Spokane's condition worsened, and he had to be destroyed at Miles City."

Berkeley Scott, writing for *The Thoroughbred Record* of March 2, 1983, stated: "The heavier weights seemed to strain the slight horse, and Armstrong sent Spokane back to the mountains where he died shortly thereafter. He sired several winners for his owner, but did not make a lasting impression as a sire...Armstrong had a pair of cuff links made from Spokane's eye teeth, which he wore proudly until his death in the mid-1890's."

Helen Fenton, for the Butte *Montana Standard* on August 22, 1974, related the story told her by George Hungerford of Sheridan, Montana, who claimed to have owned Spokane during the last two years of the famed flyer's life.

Spokane, perhaps shipped back to Montana in September of 1897 with Marcus Daly's string, was reputedly injured in a railroad mishap. Taken off the train at Miles City, Montana, Spokane was to be "mercifully killed". Instead, he was taken to a nearby ranch where he recuperated.

Hungerford contended that when the Miles City ranch failed, the Elling Bank of Virginia City, Montana, foreclosed. The stock, including the horses, was taken to the Valley Garden Ranch on the Madison River, near present-day Ennis, Montana. This action, Hungerford stated, occurred in about 1912 or 1913.

Quoting Mr. Hungerford, the *Montana Standard* report reads: "...He (Spokane) was given to me on my seventh birthday in 1914.

"He had lost his chestnut color,...and was pretty much what you call a strawberry roan, more white than chestnut. He had one white foot. I owned him two years before he died in January of 1916.

"He was pretty well stove up from his injury. His shoulder had a big sunken place in it you could stick a finger in. He couldn't run, but he had the desire. You'd get him with other horses, and he wanted to run all the time. He really wasn't a kid's horse."

In this account, one error is apparent. Spokane had a stripe on his face and two long white stockings, not one. On the other hand, the *Louisville Courier-Journal* noted on June 24, 1889, ". . .his (Spokane's) coat looks now a little more roan than chestnut."

Those inclined to accept Hungerford's story allow Spokane to attain the venerable old age of thirty, his birth being in 1886 and his death occurring in January of 1916. Thus returned to his cradle, Madison County, Spokane remains a Montana property, the cherished gift of father to son.

The truth is that Spokane's fate remains a mystery. Or does it? Spirit horses never die. Perhaps, Spokane races the winds of eternal worlds, safely beyond the reaches of earthly mortality.

Coincidentally, the Spirit Horse did have one offspring that won a major stakes event. In 1896, a three-year-old chestnut filly by Spokane won the Cincinnati Hotel Handicap. The filly's name was Spirituelle.

****

High in the Ruby Mountains of Montana sounds the neighing of a spirit horse. His mane blown by the breeze, his head held high, and nostrils flared, he stands ready to race and win. I see him in my mind's eye, and I feel his proud presence as I stand in the shadow of his home, an imposing round barn just north of Twin Bridges. Spokane, Child of the Sun, Spirit Horse of the Rockies, born to redeem the losses of a noble race.

*****

Bibliography

BOOKS

AMUNDSON, Gary and Richard Quattlander. *General Glossary Of Terms Track Industry Program*. University of Arizona. Sept., 1981.

BARON, Randall S. and Philip Von Borries. *The Official Kentucky Derby Quiz Book*. Louisville, Kentucky: Devyn Press, 1986.

BOLUS, Jim. *Run for the Roses: 100 Years at the Kentucky Derby*. New York: Hawthorne Books, Inc., 1974.

BROWN, John A. and Robert H. Ruby. *The Spokane Indians: Children of the Sun*. University of Oklahoma Press, 1982.

BRYANT, Beverly and Jean Williams. *Portraits in Roses: 109 Years of Kentucky Derby Winners*. New York: McGraw Hill, 1984.

CLARK, Kenneth. *Animals and Men*. New York: William Morrow and Co., Inc., 1977.

CHEW, Peter. *The Kentucky Derby: The First One Hundred Years*. Boston: Houghton-Mifflin, 1974.

The Churchill Downs Centennial Kentucky Derby Book, 1875-1974. Ed. Bob Gorham. Louisville, KY: Churchill Downs (privately printed), 1973.

DURHAM. "The Wright Campaign." *Durham's History of Spokane and the Inland Empire*. S. J. Clark Publishing Co., 1912.

Farley, John. *Inland Empire: D. C. Corbin and Spokane*. Seattle: University of Washington Press, 1965.

FULLER, George W. "Steptoe Disaster" and "Wright Campaign". *The Inland Empire of the Pacific Northwest: A History*. Vol. III. Spokane-Denver: H. G. Linderman, 1928. Pp. 1-14, 15-32.

Goodwin's Official Annual Turf Guide for 1888. New York: Goodwin Bros. Pp. 232, 434, 494, 505, 511.

Goodwin's Official Annual Turf Guide for 1889. New York: Goodwin Bros. Pp. 90, 132, 135, 240, 241, 273, 301, 438, 456.

Goodwin's Official Annual Turf Guide for 1890. New York: Goodwin Bros. Pp. 207, 291, 295, 302.

Goodwin's Official Turf Guide for 1892. New York: Goodwin Bros. Pp. ccxcv.

Goodwin's Official Turf Guide for 1893. New York: Goodwin Bros. Pp. ccl.

Goodwin's Official Turf Guide for 1895. New York: Goodwin Bros. Pp. ccxxxviii.

Goodwin's Official Turf Guide for 1896. New York: Goodwin Bros. Pp. ccxiix.

The Kentucky Derby: Churchill Downs 1875-1984. Louisville, KY: Privately published by Churchill Downs.

LEACH, George. *The Kentucky Derby Diamond Jubilee Book: 1875-1949*. New York: Dial Press, 1949.

LONGRIGG, Roger. *The History of Horse Racing*. New York: Stein and Day, 1972.

MARCOSSON, Isaac F. *Anaconda*. New York: Dodd, Mead, and Co., 1957

Not in Precious Metals Alone: Manuscript History of Montana. Helena: Montana Historical Society, 1976.

PLACE, Marion T. *Mystery of Wild Horse Trap*. Caldwell, ID: Caxton Printers, 1971.

ROBERTSON, William H.P. *The History of Thoroughbred Racing in America*. Englewood Cliffs, NJ: Prentice-Hall, 1964.

TRAFZER, Clifford E. and Richard D. Sheuerman. *Renegade Tribe: The Palouse Indians and the Invasion of the Inland Pacific Northwest*. Pullman, WA: Washington State University Press, 1986.

WARNER, Ezra J. *Generals in Blue*. Louisiana State University Press, 1964. Pp. 574.

WEINRUSH, Henry L. "Big Trouble." *Indian Country: Cultural View of the Spokanes*. Minneapolis, MN: T. S. Dennison and Co., Inc., 1963.

WOLLE, Muriel Sibell. *Montana Pay Dirt: A Guide to the Mining Camps of the Treasure State*. Denver, CO: Alan Swallow, 1963.

Encyclopedia Articles

"Montana." *World Book*. 1983 ed.

"Sitting Bull." *World Book*. 1983 ed.

Periodicals

"Account of the Kentucky Derby." *Spirit of the Times.* 18 May 1889; 1.

"A Great Horse Market at Miles City." *The Northwest Magazine.* Sept. 1890; 29.

"A Few Facts About Montana." *The Northwest Magazine.* Feb., 1889; 27.

BURKE, Carleton F. "Pastime of Millions." *The Thoroughbred of California.* May, 1950; 60.

CLARKE, Helen. "Montana's Winner of the Kentucky Derby." *Western Horseman.* Nov., 1959; 41, 75-76.

"Concerning Montana." *The Northwest Magazine.* May, 1889; 14.

Death of Marcus Daly. *The Thoroughbred Record.* 17 Nov. 1900; 229.

"The Death of the veteran trainer and jockey, Tom Kiley..." *The Thoroughbred Record.* 14 March 1914; 138.

"Diamonds in Montana." *The Northwest Magazine.* May 1890; 3.

"Elemendorf." Advertisement. *The Thoroughbred Record.* 19 June 1895; 41:26:417.

"Fairhaven Stock Farm." Advertisement. *The Livestock Record.* 20 Feb. 1892; 35:4:2.

"Fred T. Counter." *The Breeder and Sportsman.* 19 March 1892; 357:3.

"George W. Scoggan Dead." *The Livestock Record.* 17 Nov. 1894; 312.

"In Montana, Helena keeps the capital..." *The Northwest Magazine.* Oct., 1890; 12.

"It is on the Marcus Daly ranch..." *The Northwest Magazine.* March 1890; 28.

"John Rodegap Dies in Louisville." *The Thoroughbred Record.* 31 May 1890; 28.

Kentucky Livestock Record. 18 March 1882; 15:166.

Kentucky Livestock Record. 15 March 1884; 19:165.

"Letter from Nashville." *Livestock Record.* 6 July 1889.

Livestock Record. 16 May 1882; 17:21:324.

Livestock Record. 18 May 1889.

Livestock Record. 25 May 1889; 326.

"Maxwelton Stock Farm." Advertisement. *The Thoroughbred Record.* 23 Jan. 1897 - 18 Sept. 1897.

"Montana." *The Northwest Magazine.* Nov. 1889; 34.

"Montana." *The Northwest Magazine.* Feb. 1890; 39.

"Montana as a Health Resort." "Seattle's Great Calamity." "Montana." *The Northwest Magazine.* July 1889; 11, 22, 25.

"Montana horses..." *The Northwest Magazine.* Sept. 1890; 30.

"The Montana Meetings." Advertisement. *The Thoroughbred Record.* 30 May 1896.

"Montana Racing." *The Thoroughbred Record.* 20 June 1896.

"Niddervale Stock Farm." Advertisement. *Livestock Record.* 7 Jan 1893; 37:1:19.

The Northwest Magazine. Oct., Nov., Dec., 1889. Aug., 1890; 11. Oct., 1890; 31. Nov., 1890; 31,32.

O'DONNELL, Jack. "The Derby of the Century." *The Elks Magazine.* May, 1931; 10.

"Phonographic Marriage." *The Northwest Magazine.* Dec., 1890; 48.

PRATT, Grace Roffey. "Lion Mountain." *Frontier Times.* Aug. - Sept., 1973.

PRATT, Grace Roffey. "Montana's Derby Winner." *Western Horseman.* Jan., 1976; 4, 101-102.

"The Precious and Ornamental Stones of Montana." *The Northwest Magazine.* Dec., 1890; 48.

QUIGG, L. E. "Life in Butte." *The Northwest Magazine.* Nov., 1889; 5, 6.

"Red Cloud's Little Joke." *The Northwest Magazine.* Aug., 1889.

REMAS, Michael. "The Derby Is the Big One." *Eagle Magazine.* May, 1971; 16-17.

RUSSELL, Eugene H. "Kentucky Derby." *The Times.* 1949.

SCOTT, Berkeley. "In a Class by Himself." *The Thoroughbred Record.* 2 March 1983; 217:9:1366.

Spirit of the Times. 9 May 1874; 301.

"The suggestion..." *The Northwest Magazine.* Dec., 1890; 38.

"Summary American Derby." *Livestock Record.* 29 June 1889; 29:26:404.

"Tammany." *The Spirit of the Times.* 5 Jan. 1901; 140:26:1.

The Turf, Field, and Farm. 10 Oct. 1873; 227.

"The Turf Gossip: Jockey Kiley on the Derby." *The Thoroughbred Record.* 18 May 1889; 29:311.

"Why Daly Retires." *The Thoroughbred Record.* 18 Sept. 1897; 46:134.

Newspaper Articles

"A different story can be heard..." *Helena Independent.* 1 June 1890.

"The American Derby." *Louisville Courier-Journal.* 22 June 1889.

"American Derby in Chicago." *Helena Independent.* 21 June 1891.

"American Derby Horses: Candidates for the Great Race at Washington Park." *Chicago Daily Tribune.* 20 June 1889.

"American Derby Horses." *Louisville Courier-Journal.* 6, 7, 9, June 1889.

The American Gentleman's Newspaper. 1873.

"A Montana Horse Again Scores Success in the Great American Derby." *Helena Daily Independent.* 22 June 1890.

"Another Derby Account: The Event Described in a Manner Peculiar to the Poetic and Redundant Fancy of Chicago Reporters." "Proctor Not First." "Spokane." *Louisville Courier-Journal.* 23 June 1889.

"Armstrong's Colts." *Helena Independent.* 28 March 1890.

"Armstrong's Discovery." *The Daily Independent* (Helena). 30 March 1891.

"Armstrong Talks About Spokane." *Louisville Courier-Journal.* 20 May 1889.

"A Spirit Horse." *The Nashville American.* May, 1889.

"Bab at the Races." *Louisville Courier-Journal.* 7 July 1889.

BANKS, Gayle. "Spokane - 100 Years Old." *Madisonian.* 12 June 1986; 113:32:14.

BIDWELL, Ralph. "Spokane, Montana's Lone Derby Winner." *Great Falls Tribune.* 7 May 1977.

"The Birth of Spokane." *Spokane Morning Review.* 8 Sept. 1889.

BROUGHAM, Royal. "The Morning After." *Seattle Post-Intelligencer.* 29 April 1948.

"Bryant Has Recovered."*Louisville Courier-Journal.* 25 June 1889.

"The Chicago Derby: Spokane and Sorrento Likely to Go to the Post as Favorites with Proctor Knott and Don Jose Next Choices." *Louisville Courier-Journal.* 20 June 1889.

Chicago Sunday Tribune. 23 June 1889.

"Daly to Quit Turf." *The Helena Daily Herald.* 10 Sept. 1897.

"Decorating Spokane: The Fund for Honoring the World Famed Race Horse." *Spokane Morning Review.* 19 May 1889.

"The Derby Described." *The Nashville American.* 11 May 1889.

"Derby Day's Double: Three-Year-Old Cracks to Meet for the Clark Stakes - the Programme." *Louisville Courier-Journal.* 14 May 1889.

"The Derby-Day Heroes." *Chicago Daily Tribune.* 22 June 1889.

"The discouraging news. . ." *Helena Independent.* 25 May 1890.

DIXON, Lucille. *Madisonian.* 1954. (Courtesy of the Virginia City Museum; Virginia City, Montana.)

"Drexel Stakes." *The Chicago Tribune.* 10 July 1889.

FAUST, Homer. "Spokane, Montana Horse Won Fame." *Tribune* of Shelby. 16 May 1932.

FENTON, Helen. "Madison County Horse Race Honors Spokane, Montana's Derby Champion." *The Montana Standard* (Butte). 22 Aug. 1974; 14.

"Game Sam Bryant." *The Nashville American.* 13 May 1889.

"Glorious Spokane." "Spokane Forever." *Great Falls Tribune.* 24 June 1889.

Helena Independent. 9 May 1938; 8.

"Honoring Spokane: The Famous Racer to be Appropriately Decorated. The

People of Spokane Falls Manifest Their Appreciation of His Wonderful Achievements." *Spokane Morning Review.* 16 May 1889.

"Horses and Horsemen." *Helena Independent.* 2 April 1890. 27 June 1890. 2 Nov. 1890. 16 Nov. 1890.

"How Proctor Knott Got There." *Louisville Courier-Journal.* 6 July 1889; 3.

"How the Sheridan Was Lost." *Spokane Review.* 9 July 1889.

"Hyder Ali." *Helena Independent.* 2 Oct. 1891.

"Kentucky Broke: A Nag Called Spokane." *Spokane Spokesman Review.* 10 May 1889.

"Life in Racing Stables." *The Daily Independent.* 21 July 1891; 2.

"Lost to the Turf: The Stallion Spokane Forever Ruined for the Track." *Seattle Press-Times.* 15 Oct. 1891;2.

Louisville Courier-Journal. 5 May 1889.

Madisonian. 18 May, 1 June, 22 June, 1889.

"Magic in the Name: Spokane Again Beats the Famous Proctor Knott." *Spokane Morning Review.* 15 May 1889.

"Marcus Daly Bought Hamburg." *Louisville Courier-Journal.* 15 Dec. 1897.

McDONALD, Claire. "Montana's Past Holds Kentucky Derby Winner." *Great Falls Tribune.* Montana Parade Section. 5 May 1957; 2, 13.

"Octogenarian Dies at Home of His Son." *Seattle Post-Intelligencer.* 22 April 1907; 9.

"Once More to the Front." *The Helena Independent.* 23 June 1889.

"Our Great State." *Great Falls Tribune.* 15 July 1889; V:53.

"Owners and Trainers Jubilant Over the Recent Rainfall." "Spokane and Derby Horses to Start in the Clark Stakes." *Louisville Courier-Journal.* 13 May 1889; 6.

"Preparing for the Great Race." *Louisville Courier-Journal.* 21 June 1889.

"Proctor Knott." *Helena Independent.* 2 Feb. 1891.

"Proctor Knott and Spokane Appear Together for the First Time This Season." *Helena Independent.* 18 June 1890.

"Proctor Knott's Departure: The Famous Gelding, with the Rest of the Bryant String, Reaches Chicago." "Shot at a Horse Race." *Louisville Courier-Journal.* 19 June 1889.

"Proctor Knott, Spokane: They Will Begin in Fine Condition." *Spokane Spokesman Review.* 28 March 1890.

"Proctor Knott, the well-known race horse died . . ." *Helena Independent.* 7 Aug 1891.

"Races at Latonia." "Congratulations Tendered by the City Council, Spokane Falls." *Spokane Morning Review.* 29 May 1889.

"Reducing His Stock." *The Helena Daily Herald.* 2 Nov. 1897.

"Royal Derby." *Louisville Courier-Journal.* 10 May 1889.

"Sam Bryant Is Happy." *Helena Independent.* 3 April 1890.

"Seattle's Eastern Fame." *Seattle Journal.* 5 Aug. 1890.

SIMON, Julie. "Derby Winner Once Trained in Bayers Barn." *Tribune-Examiner* (Dillon). 17 Nov. 1981; B:1.

"Spokane: A Spirit Horse." *Louisville Courier-Journal.* 19 May 1889; 14.

"Spokane Enterprise: A Montana Paper Thinks It Has No Equal." *Spokane Morning Review.* 5 June 1889.

"Spokane, Historic Ruby Valley Horse Won Derby on Spirits of Indian Horses." *Madisonian.* 27 Dec. 1963; 1, 5, 6.

"Spokane moved for the first time this spring. . ." *Helena Independent.* 20 April 1890.

"Spokane's New Clothes." *Louisville Courier-Journal.* 21 June 1889; 2.

"Spokane's Owner in the City and Speaks of the Great Derby Winner." *Helena Independent.* 17 March 1890.

Spokane Spokesman Review. 25 March, 12 April, 16 April, 1941.

"Spokane Repeats: Proctor Knott Far Behind This Time." *Seattle Post-Intelligencer.* 15 May 1889; No. 15.

"Spokane the Victor." *Chicago Sunday Tribune.* 23 June 1889; 9, 10.

"Straight Tips on Races." *Helena Independent.* 2 July 1891.

"Talk of the Horses." *Louisville Courier-Journal.* 3 June 1889; 6.

"Talk of the Turf." *Louisville Courier-Journal.* 27 May 1889; 8.

"They Can't Beat Him: Spokane Gives Proctor Knott Another Beating in the Clark Stake: The Montana Colt Makes the Famous Gelding Give It Up." *Louisville Courier-Journal.* 15 May 1889.

"Three Rich Stakes." *Helena Independent.* 19 Aug. 1891.

"Too Expensive." *The Helena Daily Herald.* 13 Sept. 1897.

"Topics of the Turf: Proctor Knott and His Preparation for the American Derby: The Probable Starters in the Great Event at Washington Park." *Louisville Courier-Journal.* 17 June 1889.

WADE, Horace. "Racing's Wonder Horse, Spokane, Bred Among Wild Herds of Montana Rockies, Amazed Turf World By Winning Kentucky Derby." *Police Gazette.* March 1951; 23.

"The Western Turf." *Louisville Courier-Journal.* 24 June 1889.

"Won By Proctor Knott." *The Chicago Tribune.* 5 July 1889.

"Why Spokane Was Not There." *Rocky Mountain Husbandman.* 8 Aug. 1889; 5.

Unpublished And Miscellaneous

ARMSTRONG, F. H. Personal interview. Jan., 1987.

ARMSTRONG, Herbert. Personal interview. Jan., 1987.

BAYERS, Byron. Personal interview. Aug., 1986.

BUCHINGER, P.J. Artist. Helena, MT. Spokane Colored Sketch. Courtesy of the Virginia City Museum.

BURLEW, Frederick M. *American Racing Colors: 1865-1915*. Unpublished. Courtesy of Keeneland Library. Lexington, Kentucky.

EDMISTON, Marla. Artist. Painting of Round Barn. Courtesy of State Fair. Great Falls, MT.

GOODY, Benjamin. Resident historian. Melrose, MT. Feb. 1987.

First National Bank of Spokane. Flyer. 1974.

FORD, J. A. Letter to Mr. A. M. Waddell. 13 May 1941. Courtesy of the Eastern Washington Historical Society.

HOGAN, Clio D. "History of Racing in Washington." (Matt Winn story). *The Washington Horse*. About 1950. From private records. No date available. Pp. 132, 133.

The Jockey Club of New York. Report on Belmont Stakes.

JOHNSON, Bob. Story from August, 1964. Courtesy of Spokane Public Library.

Kentucky Derby Museum Displays. "Starting Gate: The Flag Is Up." "1889 Derby." Louisville, KY; 1987.

McVEY, George. "Great Horse Spokane." Butte author. May, 1964.

MILLER, Jacob. Letters. Courtesy of Ben Goody.

Original handwritten description. Author unknown. Document presented to Charles Armstrong between 1889 and 1894.

Quinn, Frank. "Spokane Remembered." *Montana Standard* (Butte). Spring, 1975. Clipping courtesy of Devore's Saddlery of Helena, Montana.

Racing record of Spirituelle. Courtesy of *The Thoroughbred Record*.

Turner, Harriet. Personal interview. June, 1987.

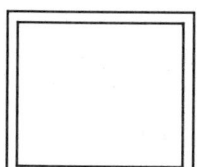 # Glossary

Allowance - weights and other conditions of a race
At stud - refers to a stallion whose services are available for siring foals
At the post - said of horses who have reached the starting area
Away - means that the horses in a race have started. They are "off" or "away."
Backstretch - straightaway furthest from the viewing stands, near the stable area
Boxed - refers to a horse racing on the rail who is confined by other horses running in front, behind, and to the side
Cannon bone - on a horse's foreleg, the area between the knee and the ankle; on its hind leg, the area between the hock and the ankle
Canter - a slow gallop or an easily won race
Chatelaine - woman's ornamental clasp worn at the waist to which is attached keys, purses, watches, etc., on a chain
Circuit - all the race tracks within a stated area
"Clean" legs - legs with no flaws
Clerk of scales - race track employee who weighs the jockeys with their tack and weights both before and after a race
Clock - the stop-watch used to time a horse's race or workout
Close - refers to the decreasing distance that often occurs in a race as the followers catch up to the leaders
Clubhouse - a semi-exclusive part of a race track
Colors - the clothing, or silks, worn by the jockey which indicate the owner for whom he rides
Cuppy - track condition where the surface is marked by the imprint of a horse's hooves; marks which are not readily covered by watering, harrowing, etc.
False start - an abortive beginning of a race where horses start to run before the starter gives the signal
Favorite - the horse considered by a majority of authorities and the public to be the most likely to win
Field - 1. all the horses competing in a race 2. for betting purposes, those horses defined by the racing secretary or the track handicapper as having the least chance of winning
Futurity - usually a race for two-year-olds in which entry is required long before the actual event, often even before the horse is born

Gait - a horse's pace; basically the walk, trot, and canter (gallop)
Gelding - a castrated male horse
Get - a stallion's offspring
Greensward - turf green with grass
Handicap - 1. a race where the chances of the competing horses are equalized through the assignment of weights   2. taken loosely, can refer to any important race since there is always an attempt to equalize the competition by the use of apprentice allowances, sex allowances, maiden allowances, and the like
Heavy track - track that is wet on the surface and soft underneath
In foal - refers to a pregnant mare
Infield - the part of the racing grounds enclosed by the track
Loafer - a horse that must be continually urged or pushed to do its best
Longshot - horse not favored or expected to win
Maiden - a horse that has never won a race
Markings - white body colorations useful in description or identification of the horse
Martingale - strap or straps fastened at one end to the noseband, bit, or reins, and at the other to the girth; used to prevent a horse from rearing or throwing its head
Odds on favorite - the horse whose odds indicate that successful bets will return less than even money
Osselets - bony growth on a horse's ankle joint or fetlock, caused by inflammation of the bone membranes; inflammation brought on externally through wounds, sprains, bruises, etc.
Paddock - 1. small field or enclosure near a stable in which horses are exercised   2. an enclosure near the track where the horses are assembled prior to a race
Paris-mutuel - early term for pari-mutuel, a system of wagering which returns successful bettors the precise amount of money risked by unsuccessful bettors, after deducting any tax and racing commission
Pigskin - a saddle
Purse - sum of money won in a race
Ringbone - arthritis in the pastern joint or coffin joint, known respectively as high ringbone and low ringbone
Route race - a race of $1\frac{1}{8}$ to $1\frac{1}{4}$ miles
Scratch - to withdraw a horse from a race in which it is an accepted entry
Selling plater - a horse that competes in selling races, usually not a horse of high quality
Splint - bony enlargements located on the cannon or splint bones; symptoms include swelling, heat, and sometimes, lameness. Commonly occurs in young horses that are strenuously worked.
Stakes race - a race where competing owners nominate their horse for participation and pay subscriptions, entrance, and starting fees, whether money or added prize is added or not
Sweepstakes - a stakes race where each owner taking part puts up a stake of money; the money is placed in a common fund which is then given as the winner's prize or is shared by several winners
Tout - one who gives race tips for profit
Trotter - horse who competes in harness racing
Tucked up - on a horse, refers to tightened flank muscles which can result from a race or workout
Up - indicates the jockey of a certain horse
Vinaigrette - a small box made of gold, silver, etc., with a perforated lid and used for holding smelling salts, aromatic vinegar, etc.

About the Author

Susan R. Nardinger, a native Montanan, is a dedicated teacher, historian, and writer. As an honor student, she received her B.A. degree in Elementary Education from the College of Great Falls in 1971, and her M.S. degree from Northern Montana College in 1981.

In addition to teaching continuously in the Great Falls Public Elementary Schools since 1975, conducting workshops in creative writing, and participating in the Montana Institute of the Arts, Susan enjoys promoting her community by assisting in the preservation of its heritage. Montana history has always played an important part in Susan's family life. Her grandparents were homesteaders, and her husband Dan's grandfather drove a stagecoach between Giltedge and Lewistown. Named the official Great Falls City Centennial Family in 1984, Susan's three sons, Phillip, age 16; Joe, age 14; and Greg, age 8, are commissioned to dig up the city's time capsule in the year 2009.

A life-long lover of horses, Susan is herself an accomplished rider having won numerous ribbons in local O-Mok-Sees, an Indian name for "games on horseback." Parade riding, too, rates as a favorite activity.

Susan's lastest offering, *Spirit Horse of the Rockies,* is a unique Centennial gift from the Treasure State. □